LEARN, IMPROVE, MASTER

LEARN
IMPROVE
MASTER

HOW TO DEVELOP ANY
SKILL AND EXCEL AT IT

Nick Velasquez

KODAWARI
PRESS

COPYRIGHT © 2020 NICOLAS VELASQUEZ
All rights reserved.

LEARN, IMPROVE, MASTER
How to Develop Any Skill and Excel at It

ISBN 978-1-5445-0891-7 *Hardcover*
       978-1-5445-0890-0 *Paperback*
       978-1-5445-0889-4 *Ebook*
       978-1-5445-0999-0 *Audiobook*

*To those who have dedicated their lives to the pursuit of mastery,
and those who are about to.*

Contents

Introduction 15

FOUNDATION

1. Principles of Learning 21
   Neuroplasticity and Specialization
   Association
   Chunking
   Automatic Processing

2. Myths and Misconceptions 29
   "Left-Brained vs. Right-Brained Learners"
   "Learning Styles"
   "Old Dogs Can't Learn New Tricks"
   "Learning Should Be Fun"
   "You Either Have It or You Don't"
   "The 10,000-Hour Rule"

PART I: LEARN

3. How to Learn (An Overview) 43

4. Explore 49
   The Principles 50
      Exploration Gives Us a Reality Check
      Exploration Helps Us Deconstruct the Skill
      Exploration Primes the Mind to Learn
      Exploration Leads to Better Questions
   The Strategies 52
      The Voice of Experience
      Ooching
      Media
      Insider's Point of View

5. Understand 57
   The Principles 59
      Input Modes
      Context
      Schemas and Previous Knowledge
      Progression
   The Strategies 61
      Break Down Information
      Make It Relevant
      Elaborative Questioning
      Connect to What You Know

6. Memorize 67
   The Principles 68
      Declarative vs. Procedural Memory
      Recognition vs. Recall

    Memory and Association
    Memory and Chunking
    Memory and Emotion
    Memory and Attention
    Memory and Repetition
    Domain-Specific Memory
    Memory of Content vs. Memory of Location

The Strategies 81
    Practice Retrieval
    Spaced Repetition
    Make Elaborate Memories
    Mnemonics

7. Practice 95

The Principles 96
    Practice vs. Repetition
    Deliberate Practice
    Massed vs. Distributed Practice
    Different Practice for Different Skills

The Strategies 107
    Embrace Practice
    Deconstruct, Isolate, Chunk, Reconstruct
    Focus on Fundamentals
    First Things (and Relevant Things) First
    Keep Practice Focused and Conscious
    Interleaved Practice
    Solo Practice
    Practice Partners
    Mental Practice
    Plan the Practice
    Build the Practice Habit

8. Bridge 127

The Principles 128

Transfer

Simulation

Rehearsal

The Strategies 132

Make It Look and Feel Real

Tweak the Rules

9. Perform 137

The Principles 138

Performance vs. Practice

Great Performances Stand on Great Practice

Performance and Mindset

The Strategies 140

Trust Your Training

Focus on What You Want, Not What You Don't Want

Stay Present

Let Go of Mistakes

PART II: IMPROVE

10. Gather and Use Feedback.. 149

The Principles 150

Process vs. Outcome Feedback

Feedback Needs to Be Timely

Feedback Needs to Be Taken Seriously, but Not Personally

Feedback Needs to Be Concrete

Feedback Needs to Be Followed by Action

The Strategies 153

Set Metrics

Prioritize What to Work On

Test
　　　The Humble Mirror
　　　Recordings
　　　Fresh Perspective
　　　Guidance
　　　Debrief, Analyze, and Document Your Work

11. Overcome Challenges 165
The Principles *166*
　　　Setbacks
　　　Impatience
　　　Plateaus
The Strategies *172*
　　　Manage Expectations
　　　Separate the Performance from the Performer
　　　Remember Past Success
　　　Slow Down, Take a Step Back
　　　Trust the Process
　　　Break Through Plateaus

PART III: MASTER

12. Elements of Mastery...183
　　　High-Level Proficiency and Consistency
　　　Sophisticated Memory and Mental Representations
　　　Experience
　　　Efficiency
　　　Unconscious Processing
　　　Refined Intuition
　　　Fluency and Flexibility
　　　Greater Distinctions and Attention to Detail
　　　Vision-Execution Connection and Unobstructed Expression
　　　Immersion in the Craft

13. **Path of Masters** 193
   Develop the Attitude of a Master to Become One
   Efficiency to Get More, Not to Do Less
   Observe, Study, and Emulate the Masters
   Join the Craft's Community
   Work with Mentors
   Do the Work
   One Day at a Time
   No Compromises
   Process Over Outcomes
   Make Progress the Main Goal
   Take Risks
   Overcome Success
   Kaizen (改善)

Closing Thoughts 217
Acknowledgments 221
About the Author.......................................225
Selected Bibliography 227

LEARN, IMPROVE, MASTER

Introduction

> In the case of everything perfect we are accustomed to abstain from asking how it became: We rejoice in the present fact as though it came out of the ground by magic.
>
> —FRIEDRICH NIETZSCHE

A young mother holds the body of her dead child across her lap. She looks down at him in a moment of overwhelming love and sorrow, her grief forever captured in stone by one of the greatest artists that's ever lived, Michelangelo Buonarroti. The details of this sculptural masterpiece, the *Pietà*, make us forget we are looking at marble. What we see instead are figures of flesh and drapery so vivid they keep our gaze fixed, awaiting their movement. It is one of the most beautiful works of art ever created.

In response to people's admiration of his *Pietà*, Michelangelo is supposed to have said, "If people knew how hard I had to work to gain my mastery, it would not seem so wonderful at all." What seemed like the product of pure genius was the result of years of labor and many more learning his craft. We tend to think of mastery as something magical or the consequence of raw "talent," but it comes from effort and dedication over many years—in most cases, a lifetime.

We usually see a master's polished performance or the refined final product of their efforts, but not the process behind it, and so we believe that what they do is beyond our capabilities. We think we don't have the talent or special abilities to do what they do. It's like watching a magic illusion. A magician vanishes a card and makes it reappear in an impossible location. As spectators, we see the end result and are amazed by it. But we do not get a glimpse at the mechanics that made it possible. If we could peek behind the illusion, we would find a process anyone can replicate through the study and practice of sleight of hand.

The same is true when watching a great quarterback playing a championship game, a virtuoso cellist giving a concert, or an inspiring speaker commanding the stage. We look at their performance, not how they developed their skills through a process that we could follow too.

This book is about that process: how to learn, improve, and master any skill. We'll look past the "smoke and mirrors" and study the method that creates the magic. We'll begin by exploring the principles of learning and common misconceptions (Foundation). Then, we'll discuss how to learn anything (part I). After that, we'll move into improving our abilities and overcoming common challenges (part II). And finally, we'll get into mastery and the path to pursue it (part III).

While everything we'll cover throughout the book stands on science, this is not a science book. I'll keep the scientific explanations, research, and studies to a minimum and present them in their simplest form. We can think of it this way: racecar drivers don't need to know all the mechanics or engineering of their cars; their focus is on mastering how to drive them. This will be our approach. We'll cover some science of how our mind works, but our main interest will be how to use it. For those interested in going deeper into the science, see the "Selected Bibliography" section at the end for referenced material.

I divided most chapters into principles and strategies, with each of these sections laid out one major point at a time. The principles are the essence behind the strategies, and once you understand them, you won't be limited to the strategies I give you—you'll be able to come up with your own. As pioneer efficiency engineer and management theorist Harrington Emerson noted, "As to methods there may be a million and then some, but principles are few. The man who grasps principles can successfully select his own methods. The man who tries methods, ignoring principles, is sure to have trouble." That said, you'll still find many strategies and tactics to have immediate actionable steps.

Whether you are taking on a new skill or already working on one, these pages will serve as a companion guide to help you learn and master your craft. I'll share with you everything I've learned through years researching and studying cognitive science, top performance, and mastery. I'll show you how to optimize your process and give you the tools to make your dream of excelling at a sport, music, art, (or anything else) a reality.

Nick Velasquez
Tokyo, Japan

FOUNDATION

CHAPTER 1

Principles of Learning

> Learning proceeds until death and only then does it stop...Its purpose cannot be given up for even a moment. To pursue it is to be human, to give it up to be a beast.
>
> —XUN KUANG

Learning is the greatest power of the human mind. Everything we've built, everything we've created, everything we've become has been the result of our ability to learn. And this great power is inherent in all of us. We are made to learn.

Throughout millennia of evolution, we developed two primary systems to adapt to our environment. One is our genes, a transgenerational long-term memory encoded in our DNA. Genes carry the instructions for our physiology (and some behavioral traits) and are an inflexible system that evolves over many generations. The other is our learning brain, a flexible system that learns from our environment and adapts to changing circumstances.

Our learning brain allows us to develop skills based on specific needs and wants within our lifetime. Consider reading and writing. Written language is too recent for humans to have evolved a brain structure designed for it. We can read and write because our brain can learn. And the same goes for playing a sport, a musical instrument, or a board game. Without a learning brain, we couldn't take on any of those skills, or the thousands that exist as hobbies and professions. But how does the brain learn? What's behind the greatest of our powers? Let's delve into the principles of learning.

Neuroplasticity and Specialization

The first principle we'll discuss is our brain's capacity to adapt, known in scientific terms as "neuroplasticity." Instead of being a fixed structure, our brain can change itself depending on circumstances and redirect functions to different regions to optimize the neural pathways we frequently use. The implication of neuroplasticity in learning skills is that our brain changes as we learn them. If we take on the cello, for instance, the area of our brain responsible for finger movement in our fingering hand will enlarge and become more active. With extensive practice, our brain will recruit more neurons for the task, strengthening connections and building complex networks that specialize in playing the instrument.

This principle is illustrated by the results of brain scans done on musicians. A study led by Thomas Elbert from the University of Konstanz in Germany showed that the brain area responsible for left-hand movement in violinists and other string instrument musicians, their fingering hand, was larger than in non-string instrument players.

At the same time, the results showed that the brain area responsible for right-hand movement in the same string instrument musicians, the bow hand, was similar to that of non-string instrument players. In other words, the brain area controlling the fingering hand of violinists, cellists, and bassists was overdeveloped, while the one responsible for the bow was average.

The results indicate that the string instrument musicians were not born with more complex brain structures for using their hands—had that been the case, they would have shown larger brain areas for both of them and not just one—but instead, that their brain had changed in response to the demands and use of their fingering hand, directing more energy and resources to the area responsible for its movement.

Our brain's capacity to change itself also applies to mental skills. Professor of Cognitive Neuroscience Eleanor Maguire and her colleagues examined the brain structure of London cab drivers and compared them to non-cab drivers of the same age group. Cab drivers in London must go through extensive training to navigate the city. They need to memorize streets, buildings, routes, and by the time they complete their training, they should know the fastest way from any point in the city to another. Their skill is impressive, and so is the way developing it changed their brain. Maguire and her team found that the cabbies' posterior hippocampi, responsible for spatial navigation skills, was much larger than in non-cab drivers.

Their study also revealed a direct correlation between the time spent working as a cab driver and the size of the brain area recruited for spatial navigation skills. The longer their career behind the wheel, the bigger the area used for the task. This brings us to a fundamental principle of learning and mastering skills. When we practice, our brain changes to specialize, and the more we practice, the more pronounced the effect. Let's take a closer look at how this specialization is built and strengthened.

Imagine you are on a hike, and you come across a field of high grass. There's no path ahead, so you have to make your way through this grass to cross to the other side. The next day, you go on the same hike and face the field again, but this time you see a trail of tamped-down grass made by the steps you took the day before. You follow the same route, and in doing so, you make it more accessible to walk next time. If you keep doing this for several days, that rough trail will turn into a smooth path.

Neural pathways work in a similar way. First, we create a primary neural connection for a behavior or thought process, the rough trail going from one neuron or group of neurons to another. But as we keep using the connections, they become faster and stronger, allowing information to move more efficiently from one side to the other.

Without getting too technical, this efficiency builds as a substance called myelin surrounds the neural connections we repeatedly use—a process called myelination. Myelin works as an insulator that supports stronger and faster signal exchange between neurons. The amount of myelin surrounding neural connections depends on the frequency of use. The more we use them, the more layers of myelin they get.

Myelination is the internal process for getting better at anything: through practice, we build layer upon layer of myelin on the neural pathways related to our skill, making them robust and specialized, the neural equivalent of turning a rough trail into a path. And if we continue our practice over the years, that path evolves into a speedway.

So far, we've discussed how learning promotes physical changes in our brain. Now let's see how learning changes the way we think.

Association

Learning is about making connections. Neurologically, these happen when neurons get excited simultaneously, making them bond to each other—a process first described by neuropsychologist Donald Hebb as *"neurons that fire together wire together."* Cognitively, they happen when we associate ideas, concepts, patterns of thinking, and behavior.

Let's take speaking a language as an example. We started learning our native language by making associations between sounds and our environment. The sound "mom" (or *"mamá,"* or *"maman,"* in Spanish and French respectively) was just noise, but after training from our parents, we began to associate the noise with our mother. Over time, the connection got reinforced and turned both the word and its meaning into a single unit. "Mom" stopped being noise and became permanently linked to what it represents.

Throughout life, we make thousands of these associations between noises and concepts, developing fluency in our native language. These connections become so strong we can't separate them. If someone is talking to us in our native language, we can't help but interpret concepts and meaning instead of hearing noises.

Association plays a primary role in developing skills. When learning to play the piano, for instance, we create connections between finger movements and sounds we want to produce. In hockey, we associate how we hit the puck with where we want it to go. And the same applies for other sports, arts, or anything else. We build our abilities by creating connections and reinforcing them over time.

Chunking

When associations grow complex, they lead to chunking. This is when our brain groups and processes several pieces of information as a unit instead of individually. When reading, for instance, we look at letters but process them in groups as words. Two associations are at play here: one between each letter and its sound, and a larger one for what they mean and sound like when put together to form words. Taken one step further, we chunk words together and interpret them as sentences.

When learning to drive, making a turn seems like a long list of tasks that need to happen in close succession: use the flasher to signal the turn, reduce your speed, check your mirrors, verify the road is clear, rotate the steering wheel, adjust speed as you turn. At first, each step stands on its own—*one, two, three*—and we create separate connections between each step and how our body should move. But with practice, we chunk the steps together until turning becomes one fluid sequence. We no longer process all the steps of the turn individually but see them as part of a larger action.

The same principle applies to all other learning. We start by making individual associations between concepts and behavior and then group them to form more complex, larger chunks. As we get better at processing these associations, they move from our conscious awareness into our subconscious (we no longer read letters but see words instead, and we pay little attention to our body movements as we drive). Let's take a look.

Automatic Processing

When we reinforce connections between thinking patterns or behavior, they start becoming automatic. Consider walking, a skill we learned early in life. At the time, it was difficult for us, but we don't pay attention to it now. Walking became a seemingly automatic process. We no longer think of how or in what order to move our legs and balance our body.

With enough practice, we can automate tasks, or parts of them, and reduce the conscious awareness we give to their execution. This automation is valuable in learning because it frees up conscious energy to work on other things and build on top of what we already know.

Masters take this process to the extreme. They practice their craft to a point where they can execute outstanding technique without thinking much about it. Their conscious mind is not occupied with the mechanics of the task and can instead focus on higher-order thinking, such as expression, creativity, or strategy.

Consider the speed of professional violinists. They move four fingers from one hand through the fingerboard, landing on the right position at the right time, while the other hand moves the bow at the correct angle with the right speed to get the desired sounds. That's too complex for the conscious mind to process.

Professional violinists can play fast because they have reinforced the neural connections associated with the mental and physical tasks of playing the instrument to the point of automation. They no longer focus on where to put their fingers or what angle to move the bow to hit the right notes. With the subconscious handling those parts, the violinists' conscious energy can be directed to their interpretation and other areas of their performance.

An important note to keep in mind is that automatic processing (aka automaticity) does not discriminate between desired behaviors and undesired ones. If we repeat bad habits or keep making the same mistakes, that's what we'll reinforce and automate—and they will be harder to correct later on. We must be careful, then, of what we automate to avoid transferring the wrong things into our subconscious.

———

The principles we've covered—neuroplasticity, specialization, association, chunking, and automation—are the foundation of all learning. Our brain rewires itself through practice, creating clusters of neural connections composed of associations between thoughts, feelings, and behaviors that specialize in what we repeatedly do. When reinforced, these connections move from our conscious awareness to our subconscious, becoming almost automatic. Then, our conscious mind is free again to process new tasks and add complexity to our growing abilities. Whether we go into French cooking, sculpting, or golf, these are the processes taking place behind the scenes as we learn. And they change the way we think as much as they change the physical structures of our brain.

Let's move on now to dispel the popular myths and misconceptions surrounding learning and mastering skills.

CHAPTER 2

Myths and Misconceptions

> Repetition does not transform a lie into a truth.
> —FRANKLIN D. ROOSEVELT

"Learning should be fun." "Old dogs can't learn new tricks." "You either have it or you don't." "It takes ten thousand hours of practice to master any skill." These ideas have been repeated so often they are now accepted as truth. But they are myths and misconceptions, and believing them can hurt our progress, give us a poor perception of our capabilities, and even keep us from learning something in the first place. Let's take a moment, then, to dispel the most popular but false beliefs about how we learn and what it takes to master a craft.

"Left-Brained vs. Right-Brained Learners"

Our first stop is the idea that each brain hemisphere is responsible for specific thinking modes. It's common belief that the "left brain" is responsible for logical tasks while the "right brain" is in charge of creativity. That's not exactly the case. Though one hemisphere may take priority over the other in certain thinking processes, we use *both* sides of our brain for almost everything, including learning. That means none of us are "left-brained" or "right-brained," and we shouldn't buy into learning "techniques" that target our "dominant" side or block our "non-dominant" one.

And as long as we are discussing the brain, let's get rid of another myth that's been a part of pop psychology for decades: "We only use 10 percent of our brain." It's a fantasy idea that makes for a good story, but it's not true. Brain scans, neuro-imaging, and research on brain damage, among other studies, have proved time and again that we use all brain areas and that they are often active.

"Learning Styles"

This is the idea that each of us has a primary learning style, and that we learn best when material is presented in alignment with it. Many theories have stemmed from this concept. Without getting into details, for they are beyond our discussion, a well-known example is the "VAK/VARK learning styles" theory, which categorizes learners into either visual, auditory, (reading), or kinesthetic. Another one is the Honey-Mumford model, which divides learners into activists, reflectors, theorists, and pragmatists. While all these theories propose different "styles," they share the idea that we learn best if we study based on our dominant one, a premise unsupported by research.

These theories come from observation and "experience" in classrooms, not from rigorous testing. There's no evidence that we learn better if new material is presented in what we think is our style of learning. When psychologist and cognitive scientist Harold Pashler and colleagues* set out to test the claims of different "learning styles" theories, they couldn't find any supporting studies, and instead found ones that contradicted them.

What's true is that we do have *preferences* in the way we learn, though this doesn't mean our preferred style makes the most difference in our learning. Other factors, such as the type of subject we are studying, how we perceive ourselves and our capabilities, prior knowledge, and our ability to extract underlying principles from the material, play a far more important role in how we learn.

Limited research exists on learning style theories, so even if some have validity, there's currently no thorough research to support them. In that sense, we cannot write them off as a myth, but we cannot structure our learning based on them either, much less define ourselves by their categories.

"Old Dogs Can't Learn New Tricks"

Years ago, it was thought that the brain was flexible during our development years, (childhood and early teens), and mostly rigid throughout adulthood. In other words, that we were better learners early in life. This old idea has been proven wrong. Though our brain's flexibility does decrease with age, it keeps its ability to learn and rewire itself throughout our entire lives.

What does get worse with age, however, is how good we are at *rote learning*, repeating information over and over until we commit it to memory. But rote learning is inefficient for

---

* Mark McDaniel, Doug Rohrer, and Robert Bjork.

memorizing in the first place—more on this in chapter 6. We'll explore more effective memory strategies that aren't age dependent, so we shouldn't be concerned with our diminished ability to rote learn later in life.

Despite the scientific findings, it still seems like young people learn faster. But the explanations are found in psychology and behavior rather than biological differences in age. One factor has to do with our mindset: if we believe we are too old to learn, it will have an adverse placebo effect, aka "nocebo effect," hurting our confidence and progress as long as we believe it to be true.

Another explanation has to do with our priorities and motivation. For most adults, learning comes behind work, family, finances, and other responsibilities. But for many young people their hobbies come first—be it skateboarding, playing drums, or video games—and they dedicate them as much time as possible. That extra study, practice, and attention accounts for a great part of what seems like better learning capabilities.

A different comparison we often make is with kids. We believe them to be great learners, but considering that it is their main, if not the only, responsibility and that they spend all their time learning both at home and in school, they are not better at it than adults.

The example most people like to bring up is how "quickly" they learn a language. But in reality, it takes kids several years of life to develop fluency in their primary language. And keep in mind that they are surrounded by it all day every day, and that they *need* to learn it to get by in life. That timeframe is not different for adults. With proper teaching, dedication, and a supportive environment, adults can learn even the most difficult languages in under two years.*

None of this is to say that age doesn't play any part in learning. It does. Depending on how far you want to take certain skills, you'd better start early, when your body and mind are more adaptable. If you want to be a top ballet dancer, for instance, it makes a difference to start as a kid. You can still learn the skill at any age, even become great at it—within the boundaries of your physicality—just don't expect to grace the stage of the Bolshoi Theater if you start late in life.

"Learning Should Be Fun"

Many books and articles on learning claim that learning *should* be fun. Not true. Learning *can* be fun, but it's not required to be so. Learning is challenging; it makes the mind work hard, and that isn't always enjoyable. At different points, the learning process will be dull, frustrating, and even discouraging. As Aristotle once noted, "Youths are not to be instructed with a view to their amusement, for learning is no amusement, but is accompanied with pain." That's the process. We have to embrace it and strive forward with perseverance, even when it's painful. In that sense, the condition we should be after is *enthusiasm*, not fun. We must be eager to learn, accepting the hardships that will come with it.

This doesn't mean you shouldn't enjoy learning. Have fun learning your craft, but don't rely on it being enjoyable to

---

* Acquiring foreign accents is a different skill that has to do with phonetics and speaking cadences. Compared to kids and teenagers, adults have more difficulty acquiring foreign accents for reasons beyond the discussion of this book, but which are unrelated to our biological capacity to learn.

stick to it, and don't get discouraged when it's not. Struggle is a normal part of the process, and as we'll discuss later, it even strengthens our learning.

"You Either Have It or You Don't"

We like to think that potential is determined by innate traits, that top athletes and performers got to their level because of natural advantages, and that we could do the same if we had them too. This belief protects our ego. We get to blame our shortcomings on factors beyond our control. But talent and intrinsic traits play a limited role in learning and mastering skills. How far we go in our craft is mostly under our control if we are willing to work for it.

This doesn't mean you can be anything you want. I can't tell you that. But I also can't tell you where your limits lie based on your aptitudes and perceived talents (or lack of them). No one can. What's certain is that passion and perseverance, what psychologist Angela Duckworth calls "grit," will make you great at your craft regardless of innate traits. How great? The only way to find out is by going through the process and putting in the work. In the words of the philosopher Friedrich Nietzsche, "There exists in the world a single path along which no one can go except you: whither does it lead? Do not ask, go along it."

An example to follow is that of Demosthenes, the great statesman and orator of ancient Athens. He was afraid of public speaking and had a speech impediment earlier in life. But through years of dedicated practice, he honed his speaking skills and became one of the best orators of his time, despite what seemed like crippling disadvantages.

Like Demosthenes, all masters had to spend countless

hours learning and refining their craft regardless of their aptitudes or "talents." No exception. None. Ever. Even Mozart, who has been popularized as a born musical genius, had to work hard to develop his skills. "It is a mistake to think that the practice of my art has become easy to me." Mozart said to the conductor leading rehearsals for *Don Giovanni*, "I assure you, dear friend, no one has given so much care to the study of composition as I. There is scarcely a famous master in music whose works I have not frequently and diligently studied." Attributing Mozart's mastery to innate abilities is a disrespect to the lifetime of dedication he put into his craft.

Expertise and expert performance studies in many fields show that innate traits and abilities have limited effect in developing excellence.* The exceptions are physical qualities such as height and body structure, but they only matter in a few areas—mostly specific sports—and only to an extent. And even in those domains, people with natural advantages still have to work hard to become great. In other words, *masters are made, not born.* As German writer Johann Wolfgang von Goethe put it, "Everyone holds his fortune in his own hands, like a sculptor the raw material he will fashion into a figure. But it's the same with that type of artistic activity as with all others: We are merely born with the capability to do it. The skill to mold the material into what we want must be learned and attentively cultivated."

Let's take basketball as an example, one of the few fields in which natural traits have a larger influence. The game gives an advantage to tall players, but being tall does not mean you are automatically good at it, nor are the tallest players the best ones. A good reference is Stephen Curry, who is several inches

---

* Many of these studies are compiled in *The Cambridge Handbook of Expertise and Expert Performance*.

shorter than the average NBA player and yet one of the best to step onto the court.

Learning and mastering basketball takes years of dedicated training, not just height. Basketball *skills* like ball-handling, shooting, passing, and rebounding have little to do with being tall. A seven-foot stature may be an advantage, but it's not necessary for developing the skills that make up the game. Those can be learned by anyone. And if basketball had height divisions, like fighting sports have weight classes to account for physical advantages, there would be top-ranked players of all heights for any playing position. They would just belong to different divisions.

Whether we're talking about basketball, public speaking, or any other skill, the most relevant impact that talent and natural abilities may have in our development is how thinking about them affects our psychology. In the book *Mindset: The New Psychology of Success*, one of the most influential works in personal development, Carol Dweck discusses how a "fixed mindset," the belief that we are born with certain qualities that can't be altered, creates a mental block that limits our thinking and our progress. But embracing a "growth mindset," the realization that we can change and get better regardless of our qualities, will motivate us to take on more significant challenges and help us improve faster.

Our mindset toward our natural abilities (or lack thereof) is crucial early in the learning process. Many people quit a new skill within weeks, believing they lack aptitude for it and can't do anything about it. They buy into the "you either have it or you don't" myth. But showing early ability is not a guarantee of anything. Some people learn faster at the beginning and then slow down. Others go through it in reverse: they have a hard time at first and progress quickly later. Learning and mastering a skill is a long-term process; a fast or slow start doesn't determine how far we'll go.

We must also keep in mind that natural abilities come in different forms. We don't know how our strengths and their combination will shape our development. Maybe we are not suited for some parts of our craft, but we may compensate in others. A musician with an average technical aptitude for classical interpretation can excel at composing or improvising. Or in the case of Steph Curry, his shooting skills—which are among the best in the game's history—more than make up for his height disadvantages in other parts of the sport.

Like basketball, most domains are composed of several parts and sub-skills, and a lacking aptitude for some doesn't mean we can't excel at the craft in general. Talent in areas like strategy, leadership, and creativity to name a few can compensate for our lack in others, including technical prowess.

All points considered, we should stop obsessing about natural abilities and focus on the things within our control, which incidentally matter most: the dedication and perseverance we put into improving our skills.

"I wasn't naturally gifted in terms of size and speed; everything I did in hockey I worked for," says hockey great Wayne Gretzky. And from the intellectual domain, we can turn to the words of Alexander Hamilton, "Men give me credit for some genius. All the genius I have lies in this, when I have a subject in hand, I study it profoundly," he said. "Day and night it is before me. My mind becomes pervaded with it. Then the effort that I have made is what people are pleased to call the fruit of genius. It is the fruit of labor and thought." In the search for mastery, being talented or suited for a craft is an advantage, but in most cases, it's not a requirement.

"The 10,000-Hour Rule"

The 10,000-hour rule is a misconception popularized and echoed by high-profile authors in recent years. The idea is that it takes 10,000 hours of practice to reach mastery in any field. It makes for a marketable soundbite, but it's not true. The "rule" is a misrepresentation of research findings from K. Anders Ericsson, an authority on deliberate practice and expert performance. Ericsson himself wrote about his dissatisfaction with how these authors presented his findings. What his study focused on was the practice habits of a group of musicians (violinists to be precise) from a prestigious music school, revealing that, on average, the amount of deliberate practice accumulated by the best of them was close to 10.000 hours.

Let's take it one piece at a time. First, the study was done on a particular skill, not across many. Second, it reported an average; it did not intend to set a universal mastery timeline. Third, it looked at *deliberate* practice, a form of training requiring focus and pushing one's limits—not to be confused with mere repetition, or mindlessly going through the motions. Fourth, the study did not imply that it takes 10,000 hours to become a master—even if the time is spent in deliberate practice. Ten thousand hours was the average that the best musicians had spent in solitary, deliberate practice by the time they were twenty years old. They were excellent and likely on their way to becoming the best in their field, but they still had a long way to go. Last and most importantly, Ericsson's conclusions focused on the fact that all the best musicians in the study had gone through extensive hours of deliberate practice, suggesting that talent had little to do with developing their exceptional skills.

Let's set the record straight. What the study found was not that it takes 10,000 hours of practice to become a master in any field, but that it takes massive amounts of deliberate practice to become very good at a craft—with or without "natural advantages." People talking about the 10,000-hour rule as a mark for reaching mastery are not only misinterpreting Ericsson's findings but also focusing on the wrong thing. It's not about how long it takes; it's about how far deliberate practice can take us. In Ericsson's words, "There is no reason not to follow your dream. Deliberate practice can open the door to a world of possibilities that you may have been convinced were out of reach. Open that door."

In this chapter, we discussed some popular myths and misconceptions about learning and mastery—from the misguided expectation that learning should be fun to the limited part that age and innate traits play in developing our skills. These false beliefs won't hold us back anymore. We are now ready to learn, improve, and ultimately master our craft. So, how do we do it? Let's find out.

PART I

LEARN

CHAPTER 3

How to Learn (An Overview)

> Learning is not attained by chance, it must be sought for with ardor and attended to with diligence.
>
> —ABIGAIL ADAMS

When looking to learn a new skill, we pick up a book, watch videos, or take a class. What we don't do is spend time learning how to learn in the first place, and that's a mistake. Meta-learning (learning how to learn) should be the skill that precedes all others. Knowing the principles and strategies of effective learning will maximize the time and energy we put into anything else, as well as optimize our work in improving and mastering our chosen craft. So, how should we learn? Let's take an overview of the learning process and examine the model we'll follow to make the best of it.

It all starts with *exploring* the craft we want to learn. What's involved? How does it work? Where to begin? Think of this exploration stage as information gathering. We'll read about the skill, watch videos, go to an introductory class, talk to people already practicing it, and watch masters performing it. At this point, we are not concerned with learning or memorizing any information. Our only goal is to have a good idea of what we are getting ourselves into.

Through exploration, we'll also get to deconstruct the skill. All crafts are the sum of sub-skills, techniques, and bits of knowledge. Some build on each other. Others are independent. Some are essential, and others optional. Once we know these pieces and how they fit into the big picture, we can start working on one (or a few of them) at a time using the steps below.

First comes "**learning what to do.**" Think of this phase as studying the cognitive side of things. If we get into poker, for instance, we first have to learn some theory—rules, hands, betting—before going into the practice.

Two steps take place in this learning stage: *understanding* and *memorizing*. Though related, they are different cognitive processes that need individual attention. Understanding is about making sense of information and memorizing is about internalizing it. We can understand everything taught in a book, video, or lecture, for instance, yet not remember most of it days later. In the same way, we can memorize the information without understanding it. Both scenarios are limiting. Effective learning requires that we understand *and* memorize what we study, at least to a degree, as we move into practice.

From "learning what to do," we go into "**learning *how* to do it.**" Think of this phase as the practical side and application of the theory we studied in the steps before. Here's where we develop our abilities through *practice*. We'll work on a few pieces of our craft at a time and progressively put them together. This phase is the essence of learning any skill, and it's where we'll put most of our time and effort.

As an extension of practice, we'll go through *bridging* (simulations or rehearsals). This step is meant to transfer the skills we developed in the context of practice to the context of execution. Think of it as a progression toward performance—going from learning *how to do something* to *doing it*. Bridging is still practice, but it's made to look and feel as if we were performing, so we are better prepared for the moment we have to.

After "learning how to do it" comes "**doing it**." Here's where we put into action all our learning and practice. "Doing it" is the execution, *performing* the skill. If you are learning to sing, this would be singing for your own enjoyment or for an audience. If learning to paint, it would be working on a painting. If you are in martial arts, it could be a friendly match or taking part in a competition. Any scenario where we are using our skills is the performance, whether we are alone and doing it for our own enjoyment, in competition, on a stage for the world to see, or anything in between.

When we perform, we are not actively trying to learn. Instead, we want our training to flow through us unobstructed, and that requires us to focus on executing our skill rather than trying to improve it. Even though performance is not and *should not* be aimed at learning, it supports it indirectly by reinforcing what we already know and providing us with valuable feedback.

In essence, the process goes like this: We begin by exploring our chosen craft to get an overview and identify the parts that compose it. Next, we work on one or a few pieces at a time, first understanding and memorizing the concepts behind them, and then going into practice to transform the knowledge into abilities. Whenever possible, we'll include simulations and rehearsals to work as a bridge between practice and execution. And finally, we take all our training and put it to use as we perform to the best of our ability, an indirect learning step that reinforces what we've worked on and provides us with feedback.

Let's see the process in action. Imagine we are going into cooking. After an exploration, we decide to start by building our knife skills, an essential element of cooking and a great place to start. Among the different knife techniques, we'll take chopping (cutting ingredients into bite-size pieces) as our example.

Keep in mind that we don't learn a craft as a whole; we build it piece by piece. In that sense, we don't learn "cooking," because that's only a term encompassing a series of principles, sub-skills, and techniques. Chopping is one such technique, and we would then apply the same learning process to all the others and progressively put them together to build what we recognize as the skill and art of cooking.

Learning to Chop

Knowing what to do: For this phase, we could take a cooking class, read an explanation, watch a video, or have someone show us how to chop. That takes care of *understanding* the steps. Then, we need to *memorize* them. We have to internalize the knowledge, so we can minimize the times we'll interrupt practice to restudy.

Here are the steps:

- Grip the base of the knife's blade with your index finger and thumb and wrap the remaining fingers around the handle.
- Hold the ingredient with the index, middle, and ring finger of your other hand—middle finger slightly forward, and the other two behind—and keep them perpendicular to the cutting board.

- Guide the blade along the flat surface between the knuckles of your middle finger as you push it down and slightly slide it forward to cut.

Knowing how to do it: Now that we understand and remember the steps, we'll *practice* them. Here's where we take the concepts we learned above and turn them into an actual skill (turning chopping knowledge into chopping skills).

Once we feel comfortable with the technique, we can set up practice scenarios that simulate real performances. If our goal is to work at a restaurant, we could simulate "rush" hours by increasing our speed and chopping different ingredients with difficult sizes and shapes. That would be our form of *bridging,* a way to progressively prepare for using our skill under performance conditions.

Doing it: This is the execution of our new skill—either for cooking at home or in a professional kitchen. Though we are not learning directly in this phase, we are reinforcing our technique and getting feedback to improve it.

Understand, memorize, practice, bridge, perform. That's the process for learning anything. In the following chapters, we'll go in depth into every part discussing principles and strategies to optimize them.

The individual attention we'll put into each learning step may give the impression that they happen (or should be approached) separately or in a rigid sequence, but we are only isolating them to build a progressive understanding of how to learn. In reality, we may jump from practice back to memorizing because we forgot something or leap straight to performance without time for bridging. The steps and the order in which we'll discuss them are only a conceptual guideline; in application, we'll mix them and move from one to another depending on the need.

In this chapter, we took an overview of the learning process and the different steps in it. Let's now move on to discuss the first of those steps in depth: exploration. We'll *explore* our chosen craft and discover what's involved, how it's practiced, and what it takes to become good at it. Our goal will be to get a realistic view of what we are getting into and start mapping the path ahead. Let's explore.

CHAPTER 4

Explore

First tell yourself what kind of person you want to be, then do what you have to do.

—EPICTETUS

What draws us to learn a new skill? Most of the time it's seeing the work or performance of those who are great at it. We see their abilities in action and fantasize about how good it would feel to be the ones doing it. But we are only looking at a part of the picture, *the performance*, and not the years of study, practice, and effort behind it. To get the full picture, we need to explore the craft: learn how it's practiced, what it comprises, and what it takes to excel at it. We must know its challenges, pleasures, and pains. Without that knowledge, we can't know if it's really what we want to pursue. But how does this exploration phase work? And what can we do to get the most out of it? That will be the subject of this chapter.

Note: This chapter is for those new to a craft. If you have been learning yours for some time, you already know what it entails. In that case, exploration can expand your understanding or help you renew your motivation to keep improving, but feel free to jump ahead to the next chapter.

THE PRINCIPLES

Exploration Gives Us a Reality Check

Many people take up the guitar, drums, or other instruments with the dream of playing live in front of a cheering audience. They imagine how good they would look playing on stage and making the crowd roar. But the path to that goal is usually through thousands of hours of solo practice, followed by more hours composing, refining, and rehearsing songs. Playing live usually accounts for a fraction of what's involved in playing an instrument.

We get lost in the spell of the "finished product," like watching athletes compete, musicians play a concert, or artists show their work. We are attracted to those moments and dream of getting there ourselves, but those performances are the end results of their efforts. By not looking deeper, we miss what's behind them: the endless hours of practice, the years of study, the discipline, the sacrifices, and in some skills, the physical toll on the body.

"Dancing appears glamorous, easy, delightful. But the path to paradise of the achievement is not easier than any other," said renowned dancer Martha Graham. "There is fatigue so great that the body cries, even in its sleep. There are times of complete frustration, there are daily small deaths." That's what it takes to get where we want to go. We need to know that; we need to see behind the glamour of performance.

This reality check can be demotivating, as we may realize our chosen craft is not what we were looking for or that we don't want to do the practice it requires. But knowing what the skill is about, how it's practiced, and where it can take us could also make it more appealing. The point is, we need to explore it to find out.

Exploration Helps Us Deconstruct the Skill

Exploration is also a way to discover the different parts that make up the craft. These are the sub-skills, techniques, and principles that comprise it. Learning to play the guitar, for example, involves music theory, scales, chords, picking technique, and left-hand finger dexterity, among other things. And those parts have sub-parts in turn: scales are divided into major, minor, pentatonic, and so on.

We need to deconstruct our chosen skill and become familiar with the different elements involved. Doing so will help us develop a better plan for which ones to focus on, in what order, and how to approach them. There's a lot to learn in a craft, and if we don't break it down and focus on what matters most at a given moment, we'll drown in its magnitude.

Exploration Primes the Mind to Learn

Exploration brings perspective, context, and purpose to the day-to-day learning and practice (the "grind") and how they fit into the overall craft. When we see the big picture, it's easier to stay motivated and internalize the smaller pieces and sub-skills. Let's take rock climbing, for instance. Ropework and tying knots are an important part of the sport. But if we start learning those parts without knowing their role, the information remains abstract and hard to memorize...even boring. It's when we understand their use and how they fit into rock climbing—when we see the context and purpose around them—that we become engaged and prime our mind to learn them.

Exploration Leads to Better Questions

If we are delving into writing and ask, "How do I become a good writer?" we'll get the answer, "Write a lot and read a lot." That's good advice, but it's also vague, and it is so because the question is vague. If we ask instead, "How do I energize a piece of writing?" we'll get something like, "Speed up the pace by shortening your sentences, using frequent paragraphing, and cutting most adverbs and adjectives."

That's the power of asking better questions: we get specific answers tailored to our goals and circumstances. But we can't ask them if we don't build basic knowledge first. That's where exploration comes in. With an overview of our chosen craft, we'll develop enough understanding to ask those better questions—and get better answers.

THE STRATEGIES

The Voice of Experience

A great way to start our exploration is by talking to people already involved in what we want to learn—from beginners to advanced practitioners to pros, coaches, and teachers. We'll ask them about the process and anything they can share on learning, practicing, and performing. What do they find most challenging? What mistakes should we try to avoid? What deserves special attention? Their insight will provide us with a real sense of the path ahead. At the same time, they can help us deconstruct the skill by telling us the different pieces that compose it and their level of importance. That information will give us a structure for the sub-skills and techniques we'll be learning later on.

Ooching

"Ooching" means getting a taste of what we are going into, to dip our toes before we dive. I came across the term in the book *Decisive: How to Make Better Choices in Life and Work* by Chip and Dan Heath. The idea of ooching is to try things before committing to them, such as taking a short painting class before applying to art school. Other ways to ooch would be to attend classes as a spectator or observe artists as they practice. In these options, instead of getting involved, we would be looking from the outside trying to absorb as much as we can. But the goal remains the same: develop a better understanding of the craft before we make a more significant commitment to it.

Ooching also gives us a better sense of what the day-to-day practice looks like. This is important because some skills are different from what they seem. As an example, I took flying lessons thinking that flying a plane would give me a sense of freedom. But after a few lessons, I realized it was not what I thought. What I expected to be liberating fun was replaced with attentive planning, weather analysis, communication protocols, operational checklists, and following airspace regulations. Still a good experience, but not what I was after.

On the opposite side, I thought I wouldn't enjoy surfing. I'd never had an interest in water sports, and riding a wave didn't sound like a good idea considering my let's call it *acquired respect* for water after almost drowning twice as a kid. But surfing turned out to be different from what I had imagined. I enjoyed floating in the water, appreciating nature, and feeling the waves' movement until it was time to ride the next one—and the thrill that came with it. The point is, we need to try things out to see them for what they really are.

Media

Another way of exploring our craft is through articles, interviews, books, documentaries, and videos that document a master's skill beyond the performance. We've already been exposed to the performance part many times; it's what got us interested in learning the skill in the first place. We take on the guitar inspired by great performances from guitar players we love, or we go into tennis because we want to own the court like our idols do. What we don't see often is the process behind it: someone practicing scales or working on their backhand. But at this stage, that's what we should look into.

For someone who wants to become a sprinter, this could be watching videos of how the pros train. Top sprinters make the sport look easy, but when we look at the work that goes into it, we realize how difficult and demanding it is. Usain Bolt offers us a glimpse in an interview, "I think a lot of people see you run and then they say, 'Oh, looks so easy, looks effortless,'" Bolt says. "But before it gets to that point it's hard work, it's day in and day out sacrifice, day in and day out just dying." That's what awaits any aspiring sprinter, and they better know it going in.

ME w/ Transition

Insider's Point of View

The previous strategies centered on looking "behind the scenes" rather than admiring the performance, but here, we'll do the opposite: we'll look at the performance, though we'll do so from an insider's point of view.

Imagine we sat down to watch a movie with a director, and she broke down the scenes, story, and characters for us. This would give us a different experience of the film. So even though we would be looking at the end result of the craft, the finished movie, we would get a peek into the world of directing and what goes into filmmaking.

The idea applies to any skill. We can watch a football game with someone knowledgeable in the sport's tactics and plays, listen to a political speech with a professional public speaker, or go through an art museum with an art connoisseur. The goal is exploring what we are interested in through the perspective of those who know what's happening and why.

Exploration gives us an overview of our chosen skill from study to practice to execution, and with it a good sense of whether it's something we want to pursue. Through exploration, we also identify the sub-skills and techniques that make up the craft and even take a peek at the path ahead. But this stage has been about discovery, not learning. The goal was to know better, and now that we do, we are ready to learn. How do we do it? Let's find out.

CHAPTER 5

Understand

What we do not understand we do not possess.
—JOHANN WOLFGANG VON GOETHE

Learning is most effective when we understand the principles, logic, and purpose of what we study. For this reason, understanding sits at the base of learning anything. We need to make sense of what we are doing, how it works, and why, so we can optimize the rest of the process.

Let's use an example from Brazilian Jiu-Jitsu, a grappling martial art. If we want to learn how to do an armbar, a submission technique that attacks an opponent's elbow joint, we must start by understanding the steps involved in the move.

To keep things simple, here are the five main steps (from a full guard on the right side):*

1. Hold your opponent's right arm against your torso.
2. Place your left foot on your opponent's right hip.

---

* If you want to see the armbar, you can go to UnlimitedMastery.com/armbar.

3. Bring your right leg behind your opponent's left shoulder and push him down.
4. Pass your left leg over your opponent's head.
5. Extend your body against your opponent's right elbow joint.

Before we practice the move, we should know the purpose behind it—in this case, making our opponent tap out. We should also understand the steps, their sequence, and why they matter. We control our opponent's arm (step 1), before placing our foot on his hip (step 2) because without that control our opponent can escape and even pass our guard. Next, we bring our leg behind our opponent's shoulder and push him down (step 3) to break his posture. If we don't, he'll have more balance and space to move. It will also make it harder for us to pass our leg over his head (step 4). Finally, we extend our body (step 5) to create leverage against our opponent's elbow joint and make him tap out.

Understanding the logic behind each step makes the move easier to process, memorize, and practice. It also gives us insights into the principles behind the technique, which apply to many other moves in the martial art, such as restricting an opponent's movement to trap them, breaking their posture to throw them off balance and limit their movement, and using our body as leverage to attack joints.

Understanding sets the foundation for all learning. Knowing what we must do, why it matters, and why it's done the way it's done improves all other learning phases. But what influences how we process and understand information? And how can we get better at it? That will be the subject of this chapter.

THE PRINCIPLES

Input Modes

We'll start with the different ways we take in information:

- Observation: watching someone do what we want to learn
- Imitation: following along as someone else does it
- Explanation: reading or listening as someone else breaks down the subject
- Experimentation: trying to figure things out on our own

Depending on the situation, some input modes work better than others. In learning the armbar, reading about the move or just winging it on the mat wouldn't be useful (and could get someone hurt). And the same is true in other sports: we are better off having someone guide us or following along with a video or coach. In other instances, a book or audio course might work well. It depends on what we are learning.

Whenever possible, we should mix several input modes in our learning: have a coach or teacher explain it to us (explanation), watch others do it (observation), follow along (imitation), and then experiment on our own (experimentation). Using more than one input mode will make for a stronger understanding and help with memorizing later.

Context

We learn better when we know the context of what we are studying and how it fits into the larger picture. Think of context as the image on the jigsaw puzzle box that shows you what the finished puzzle should look like. Without this guide, it would be difficult to make sense of the hundreds of pieces jumbled around your table. Or imagine how confusing it would be to study opening moves in chess without first knowing what the game is about or the rules to play it.

Context gives new knowledge structure, making it easier to understand. At the same time, it makes information more engaging. Seeing how each part of what we learn, regardless of how small, plays into the big picture makes us pay attention and study it with motivation—two essential qualities for better learning.

Schemas and Previous Knowledge

A schema is a conceptual framework made of previous knowledge and experience that helps us process new information. Let's assume you've never seen a leopard. If I were to explain it to you, I could start by naming its characteristics one by one, such as its size, weight, and that it has pointy ears, a long tail, and four legs. Or I could tell you to think of a big wild cat and then explain its unique features, like its distinctive spotted coat. The latter example is easier to understand because you are using previous knowledge—what a cat looks like—as a point of reference (schema) for understanding a new concept, a leopard.

Schemas and previous knowledge have a strong influence on learning. It's easier to leverage what we already know than to build a concept from scratch. As Aristotle noted, "All teaching and all intellectual learning come about from already existing knowledge." This is why comparisons, analogies, examples, metaphors, and parallels are great learning aids—more on this later in the chapter. On the opposite side, if we take a subject we can't relate to anything we know, we'll have to build a dedicated framework of understanding for it, making the information slower and harder to learn.

Progression

Learning anything is easier if we study it progressively—and in the right order. We need to understand basic math before we do calculus. This point sounds obvious, but we don't always approach learning this way. We jump into concepts and techniques without taking the time to build our understanding of the fundamentals—think of someone wanting to learn handstand push-ups on parallel bars before understanding the mechanics of a basic handstand.

Learning builds upon itself. We learn a piece and add to it, then add another one on top of that, and so on. Following the wrong progression will only slow us down. A guideline to keep in mind is to study from general concepts to specifics, from simple processes to complex ones, from concrete information to abstraction, and from principles to techniques and strategies.

THE STRATEGIES

Break Down Information

One of the best ways to understand something is by taking it apart and examining how its pieces fit together. What are the key elements? How do they interact? What makes it all work? Here are ways to help us deconstruct new information.

Note-taking: Taking notes—including observations, questions, and ideas—serves to elaborate on what we study. It promotes connections to other information and to what we already know, making new material easier to understand and memorize. At the same time, it helps us extract main ideas and categorize knowledge based on importance.

Self-explanation: Putting concepts into our own words and

summarizing what we study forces us to ruminate on the knowledge and condense it to its fundamental ideas. At this point, we are not concerned with memorizing yet; the goal is only to identify core elements of what we are learning and process them in terms we understand.

Concept Maps: These are a visual way to organize knowledge by drawing connections between concepts.* Our brain has greater processing power for visual stimulus than language. So, by putting information in visual terms, we improve understanding and retention. Also, drawing concept maps forces us to organize material, which on one side helps us internalize it, and on the other makes it easier to review.

Make It Relevant

As we saw with the armbar example at the beginning of the chapter, when we know the importance of each step involved and its sequence, the move becomes easier to internalize.

This is something we should look for in all learning, to go past *what* to do, and ask *why* it's done in a certain way or order. This also includes finding out how we can use or apply what we are learning and the part it plays in our craft. If we don't connect theory to application, concepts and ideas remain abstract and isolated, making them harder to process.

Our approach, then, will be to find the value of what we study and see how it contributes to the big picture. Doing so will make us more receptive to learn as well as improve our understanding of the craft and its underlying principles—which will do more for our development in the long term than focusing on what to do.

---

* For an example of a concept map go to UnlimitedMastery.com/conceptmaps.

Elaborative Questioning

Elaborative questioning is about trying to deduce the logic behind what we are learning before we are taught the answers. In the section above, we talked about the importance of knowing the "why" behind what we do. Here, we are adding a step in between. Instead of going straight to the answers, we'll try to come up with them ourselves.

In our armbar example, this would mean trying to figure out on our own why each step matters and why they follow that sequence. Even if we don't come up with the right answer, the effort we put into trying to figure it out forces us to think of the principles and the concepts behind the steps. This questioning primes our mind to learn so that, once we are given the right answer, the information becomes easier to process and takes better hold in our memory. It also has the benefit of making us scrutinize what we study instead of accepting it at face value—benefits that result in improved learning.

Connect to What You Know

We come back to using what we know to learn something new. It's an essential principle that we'll turn into an active strategy by looking for connections between what we already know and what we are trying to learn. We'll spend time thinking of how the new information relates, even remotely, to something we are already familiar with. For this, we can use analogies, metaphors, examples, and any form of comparisons—which are especially useful if they are visual and concrete.

In *The Little Book of Talent*, Daniel Coyle makes a case for thinking in images and using analogies: "Touch the strings as lightly as possible" is an example he contrasts with "Touch the strings as if they were burning hot," which is easier to interpret. Same with "Trap the soccer ball gently" versus "Let the ball kiss your foot." Analogies and visual examples such as these are the marks of great teachers. They use relatable, simple, and concrete comparisons to things we know to help us grasp new information and then expand from there.

I had the great opportunity of training Muay Thai under Mark DellaGrotte before he became a sought-after trainer for UFC fighters. Mark was the best trainer I've ever had. Aside from being an amazing teacher, he was dedicated to all his students, not just the ones showing the most promise or discipline; he wanted to get the best out of each of us.

Something that caught my attention about Mark's teaching was his use of analogies and comparisons. He related Muay Thai moves and techniques to things we already knew. At one point, Mark saw me practicing my low kick on a heavy bag and came to help me improve it. There was something off with my kick—I wasn't turning my hips enough, so it had no power. Instead of stating the logical "Turn your hips more," Mark connected the advice to something I was familiar with.

Mark knew I came from South America, where soccer is a popular sport, so he asked me if I had played before. "Of course," I said, "many times." He then told me to imagine a soccer ball inside the heavy bag and kick it as if trying to score. The comparison was visual, relatable, and easy for me to understand. My kick immediately improved. I started turning my hips without forcing the move and got more power. Mark then explained the difference in my movement and pointed out what to adjust for transferring my technique into Muay Thai. Instead of teaching me from scratch, he was helping me leverage what I already knew, making it easier to go from there. It's a great lesson to apply anywhere else.

In this chapter, we discussed how to improve the way we process and understand information. Knowing what we are trying to do, how it should be done, and why it matters is the best way to prepare for the next steps in learning. But understanding is only the beginning. We now need to find ways to keep that information in our mind, internalize it, and have it available for practice. Let's move on to the fascinating world of memory.

CHAPTER 6

Memorize

> Memory is the treasury and guardian of all things.
> —CICERO

In ancient times, learning how to remember was as important as what to remember. Memory was considered a measure of intelligence, and one of the greatest virtues someone could have, for it holds our ability to internalize knowledge. While understanding is an important step in learning, and helps with memorizing, it's only a start. Making sense of information doesn't guarantee its retention—that's why we can read a non-fiction book, understand it from start to finish, and still struggle to recount its lessons later. To internalize knowledge and get the most out of it going into practice, we need to memorize it. But how does memory work? And how can we get better at memorizing? That will be the subject of this chapter.

THE PRINCIPLES

Declarative vs. Procedural Memory

From a learning perspective, there are two types of memory: declarative and procedural. Each serves a different purpose, but both play an essential role. Declarative memory is about remembering facts, and procedural memory deals with processes—such as remembering how to drive a car or play a sport. In learning a skill, declarative memory is knowing what to do—memorizing theory, steps, concepts—and procedural memory is knowing how to do it. (In science, the difference is referred to as *knowing that* and *knowing how*, respectively.)

Different skills require a different mix of declarative and procedural memory. There's little theory involved in learning how to ride a bicycle, for instance. We rely on our procedural memory to memorize how to move our body, pedal, and keep our balance. Other skills, such as photography, public speaking, or design, involve learning more concepts—a task for our declarative memory. The focus of this chapter is on declarative memory (what to do). We'll be developing our procedural memory (how to do it) in the next chapter, "Practice."

Recognition vs. Recall

We access information in our memory in two ways: recognition and recall. Recognition is identifying something we are exposed to as something we've experienced before. It's the "Oh, I've seen this movie before" or "Oh, I've heard this song before" effect. Recall, on the other hand, requires retrieving from memory something we've experienced in the past without being exposed to it again.

Let's look at a practical example. You meet someone at a party for the first time. Weeks later, you *recognize* this person on the street but can't *recall* the name. What's happening? Recognition is an easier process for the mind. We don't need to reconstruct information from memory; we just run the input against our "database" and see if there's an existing match. *Have I met this person before? Yes, I have.*

Recalling that person's name is different. We are not hearing or seeing the name anywhere and have no input to run against our previous experience. Instead, we have to retrieve the name from long-term memory into working memory with limited help, a more complicated process than recognition. So, when people say, "I'm better at remembering faces than names," it's not only them—it's everyone. If they had to describe the new acquaintance's face without looking at it, they would find it difficult too. Recognition is easier than recall.*

The same principle makes multiple-choice tests easier than fill-in-the-blank ones. Multiple-choice questions ask us to *recognize* the answer, but when we have to fill in the blank, we are forced to *retrieve it* from memory. It's also why reviewing something we've studied in the past can feel as if we already know it—even if we don't. We recognize the material, even feel familiar with it, and it creates the illusion that we've committed it to memory. But we'll know we've memorized it only when we can recall it on our own.

---

* In addition to recognition being easier than recall, we are better at remembering visual information than language—and especially attuned to recognize faces—making all of us, unless we have brain damage, better at remembering faces than names.

Memory and Association

Memory is associative. We connect events, facts, and experiences to form webs of knowledge. This makes it possible for a single cue—partial or distorted—to trigger a series of memories. Think of when you tell a story from your past. As you move through it, you remember more of what happened. Pieces from the story trigger other memories, and those trigger more in turn. The same happens between stories: you start telling one and then remember two or three different ones. Before you know it, you've recounted several stories in a row, most times with only a detail connecting them.

This associative quality of memory is a great feature. We get to create clusters of memories and knowledge that are accessible from multiple points. It's a way of improving recall and making things harder to forget. Without it, everything we encode in our memory would exist alone with a single point of access. And if that point were lost, the memory would become inaccessible and otherwise forgotten.

Imagine there is only one road to your house. If that path gets blocked, you can't go home. (It doesn't mean your home disappeared; you just can't get to it.) But if there are many paths to it, if one gets blocked, you can take another one. Our memory works the same way. If we have only one link to a memory and it fails, we'll lose access to it. (It doesn't mean it disappeared. We just can't reach it.)* But if we have multiple pathways leading to it, we'll have more access, making it less likely to be "forgotten."

An example of the relationship between association and memory is the famous Baker/baker paradox. In a study, researchers showed two groups of participants the picture of

---

* Our memory has incredible storage capacity, and what we think is "forgotten" is many times inaccessible.

a man. One group was told that the man's last name was Baker. The other group was told that he worked as a baker. Days later, both groups were shown the picture again. Those in the name group were asked to recall the man's name, and those in the job group were asked to recall the man's job. The participants who were told his name had a hard time remembering it, but those who were told his job had more success.

The word is the same, Baker, but working as a "baker" is easier to recall. We can associate the man's image with a set of preconceptions or schemas we have about baking: cooking bread, being covered in flour, pastry smell. Our mind creates more connections, or paths, between the man's image and his job. On the other side, the name "Baker" is harder to remember because it doesn't give us much information to associate with.

This effect goes beyond remembering facts, events, or experiences; it also translates into acquiring knowledge and skills. Associating new learning with things we already know creates a larger web of knowledge that's harder to forget. So, the more connections we create between what we are learning and what we've learned before, the more likely the new knowledge will stick.

Memory and Chunking

Chunking relates to the principle of association. It happens when we group or associate several pieces of information into fewer, more manageable ones. Our short-term memory is limited and can only handle around seven pieces of information at a time and hold them for just a few seconds. Chunking keeps us from overwhelming our short-term memory by making high information volume more manageable and facilitating its transfer to our long-term memory. Let's look at an example.

Try memorizing the following letters in order:

C N N J F K T V N A S A

Now let's chunk them together and try again.

CNNJ   FKT   VNASA

Both examples have the same letters in the same order, but the second one is easier to memorize. The difference is that we grouped the twelve independent pieces of information from the first example into three chunks to contain them—a number that's more manageable for our short-term memory.

Now, if we organize chunks in a meaningful way, they become even easier to memorize.

Let's take a look:

CNN   JFK   TV   NASA

Those groups of letters have meaning to us, so by chunking them like that, they take a stronger hold in our memory. Now, if we want to go further still, we can take advantage of something our memory is especially suited for: narratives. We'll use each chunk to create a story linking them together. It could be something like this: *CNN was doing a segment about JFK on TV, but it got interrupted by a live rocket launch from NASA.* With that story, we chunked the four independent groups of information into a single one that's easy to memorize.

Memory and Emotion

Emotions are powerful for creating lasting memories. Events or knowledge that trigger strong emotional reactions are more likely to go in our long-term memory than ones that don't. Think of the most vivid memories from your life. They are full of strong emotions—good or bad. But events with no emotional charge fade into the background, too mundane to have an imprint in our memory. This is the case with what's routine and predictable. Think now of how much you remember from the time you spent commuting, showering, or checking your phone last month. Not much, if anything at all.

Emotions also have a higher priority in our mind than rational thinking. Our attention goes where our emotions go, not where our logic wants it to. Emotions have such an impact on memorizing that they are responsible for a form of extreme fast learning: the development of irrational fears and phobias. If we live a negative experience that's emotionally overwhelming, it will take immediate hold in our memory and become difficult to shake off. A kid bitten by a dog, for instance—even playfully and only once—can "learn" to fear dogs with no further exposure or repetition of what happened. The memory of the experience is so strong that it cannot even be reasoned with. That's the power of emotion. An event packed with enough emotional charge will create memories that can last a lifetime and even shape how we approach life.

While that's an extreme example, the principles at play are the same. Strong emotions create strong memories, and we can use this to our advantage. If we are passionate, interested, and engaged in what we are learning, we'll create stronger memories.

Memory and Attention

Related to the principle above is the relationship between memory and attention. We understand and memorize information better when we are engaged. But what captures our attention? Let's take a look.

We pay attention to what we consider meaningful, interesting, useful, or relevant. It's difficult to learn something we don't care about. As Leonardo da Vinci observed, "Study without desire spoils the memory, and it retains nothing that it takes in." Think of the lessons our parents tried to teach us when we were kids that started with, "This will be important when you grow up." We forgot most of them long before we needed them. Those lessons were not relevant to us and had no immediate use, so we ignored them. We cared about other things, such as learning to ride a bicycle, and when that moment came, it had our undivided attention. Whatever we consider meaningful, interesting, useful, or relevant has a magnetic effect that not only draws us in but also keeps us in.

We pay attention to what's new, outstanding, or unexpected. As we move through life, we recognize patterns and create models of the world based on them. We then expect things to be and behave the way they have in the past, and when those patterns get broken, they capture our attention.

The same goes for novelty: we get used to what we see often and stop paying attention to it, but new things attract us. It's the reason we remember a walk around a new city during a vacation but recall little from a routine walk in our hometown. The vacation breaks our day-to-day patterns and exposes us to new experiences, making us more attentive. Time seems to move slower as we live those moments—a two-week vacation feels like months' worth of memories—but it's because we are noticing more, and our memory is stimulated to record more of the experience. On the opposite side, when we follow a routine, weeks pass unnoticed. They fail to grab our attention and make a mark in our memory because there's no novelty in them.

We pay attention to what sparks curiosity. We are curious by nature. If something intrigues us, we want to dig deeper and find out as much as we can. It doesn't have to be something significant; curiosity can come even from trivial things. Addictive TV shows are a testament to that. Creators keep us locked in by making us curious about characters and plots. We become obsessed with finding out what will happen next. And though the answer won't make a difference in our lives, we can't stop paying attention. We watch episode after episode looking for relief but find another cliffhanger we "have to" resolve. Curiosity keeps us attentive for an impressive, sometimes worrisome, amount of time.

Memory and Repetition

We remember what we experience repeatedly. Through repetition (aka rote learning), we can eventually drill almost anything into our memory. But rote learning is inefficient compared to other principles for creating new memories—like association, attention, and emotion. Using repetition to memorize is like taking a wheel, laying it on its side, and then pushing it. We'll make it move and get it where we want it to go, but it's not the best way to do it.

Repetition may feel like the right approach to memory, but that's because we are used to it. We've been conditioned to memorize this way since early childhood, and it's human nature to resist changing what we've always done—especially if it works, no matter how inefficiently. This is not to say that repetition doesn't play a role in memory. It does—but not the way we've been taught. Repetition is inefficient for *creating new memories*, but it's valuable for *solidifying* existing ones.

Back in chapter 1, we discussed how our neural connections get faster and stronger through repeated use. It's here that repetition proves most useful. It helps us reinforce what we already know. Our approach for memorizing anything, then, will be to use other strategies for creating new memories (we'll discuss them shortly) and rely on repetition and repeated exposure to give them a better hold.

Domain-Specific Memory

Not long ago, the basketball star LeBron James made the news for a skill that seemed unrelated to basketball: memory. During a post-game news conference in 2018, James broke down several plays in detail as he described how the Cleveland Cavaliers allowed the Boston Celtics to rally late in the game:

> What happened? We ran them—the first possession we ran them down all the way to two on the shot clock. Marcus Morris missed the jumpshot, fouled it up, they got a dunk. We came back down, we ran a set for Jordan Clarkson, and he came off and missed it. They rebounded it, and we came back on the defensive end and we got a stop. They took it out on the sideline. Jayson Tatum took the ball out, threw it to Marcus Morris in the short corner, he made a three. We come back down, missed another shot. Then Tatum came down and went 94 feet, did a Euro step and made a right-hand lay-up, timeout. There you go.

His memory was so accurate it amazed reporters and made some speculate he had a "photographic" memory. As impressive as it seems, LeBron's memory for the game, though difficult to develop, is not uncommon for elite performers across fields. Top dancers remember complex sequences after seeing them once, skilled musicians can play chord progressions after one listen, and chess masters can play multiple games at a time in their mind—known as blindfold chess or mental chess. Through many hours of study and practice, elite performers develop a complex understanding and improved memory for their craft. They can also chunk large amounts of information into meaningful pieces that are easier to process and memorize.

We can think of elite performers' ability to chunk information related to their field using language as an analogy. While elite players see the game as words and sentences, the rest of us see it as individual letters. Let's use the sentence "He is a great basketball player" from three different perspectives as an example.

A young child who knows her ABCs but does not know how to read words will see:

H E I S A G R E A T B A S K E T B A L L P L A Y E R

That's twenty-six individual pieces of information, each *letter* in the sentence, and would be very difficult for the child to remember.

A Japanese native who is learning English as a second language (and doesn't understand the meaning of each word) will see:

He   is   a   great   basketball   player

That's six pieces of information—each *word* in the sentence—instead of twenty-six, making it easier to memorize.

Finally, let's look at it from the perspective of a native English speaker. For him, a single read of the sentence ("He is a great basketball player") is enough to lock it in his memory.

The native English speaker can memorize the statement with ease, but we cannot claim he has a better memory than the Japanese woman or the young child; he just has less information to memorize. His proficiency in English enables him to chunk the information into a single piece, the sentence.

To get an idea of the effect, imagine I asked you to memorize that same sentence in Japanese, assuming you don't know the language. Here it is (Romanized):

"Kare wa subarashī basukettobōru senshu desu."

(Actual Japanese: 彼は素晴らしいバスケットボール選手です。)

Not as easy to remember, is it?

This domain-specific memory is what's behind LeBron James's amazing memory for basketball. He doesn't see every pass or every move in isolation but as part of a larger construct. He sees a play as a whole—as a sentence, not as individual letters. The proficiency he's developed in the "language" of basketball allows him to process and memorize larger pieces of information than the rest of us.

Let's take a turn and look at chess, a game where people often see their top players as having a prodigious memory. Chess masters can remember entire boards after looking at them for a few seconds. They can recreate games they played or studied in the past and even play several games at a time in their minds. Memory in chess plays such an important role that a player's memory for the game directly links with their ability to play it well.

What's surprising is that chess masters don't have a great memory in general. They have a great memory for chess, but an average memory for other things. As with LeBron James, chess masters' amazing memory is domain specific. In psychological studies, chess masters could only keep around seven pieces of (non-chess related) information in their short-term memory—the same as most of us. Even more revealing, when asked to memorize the position of chess pieces arranged in a way that could not resemble a real game, masters could only memorize a few of them, not significantly different from lower-rank players or even non-chess players.*

Chess masters' incredible memory for the game relies on seeing, interpreting, and memorizing the relationship between pieces, not each of them individually. They look at three pieces on the board, for example, and recognize it as an attack formation they've seen in the past. They interpret it as one chunk, not three different things. So, when masters were shown pieces on a board that couldn't resemble a real game, they saw them like the rest of us: no context, no interconnectedness. That's why they had an average memory for their position.

Another important factor in chess masters' memory for the game is that they see each match in relation to the "inventory" of matches and positions they experienced over years of practice. Novices, on the contrary, don't have as many points of reference for moves or positions. They see each game as something new, making it harder to process and memorize.

---

* Original studies by Adriaan de Groot. Later repeated and expanded by other researchers, including William Chase and Herbert Simon, Neil Charness, and Peter Frey and Peter Adesman.

Here, we circle back to the influence of previous knowledge in learning or memorizing new information. In terms of our language analogy, chess masters have a more complex vocabulary and fluency for the game. They no longer see individual letters (chess pieces); instead, they see and remember words and statements grouped in relation to each other, a narrative. This allows them to chunk information on the board in meaningful ways, such as attack or defense formations, patterns, or areas of tension. And it's the reason they have a better memory for it.

The domain-specific memory displayed by LeBron James, chess masters, and other elite performers reflects the amount of study and practice they've put into their craft. They were not born with a better memory than the rest of us; they developed it through practice in their fields. It is a byproduct of the work they put into mastering their craft and carries the implication that we could achieve the same if we put in the work, too.

Memory of Content vs. Memory of Location

During the Middle Ages, information was hardly available. Books were rare, and their access limited. If you had the privilege of coming across one, you would do everything possible to memorize its content. Later, during the Renaissance, learning was aimed at the mastery of a few texts instead of shallow reading of many. Unfortunately, today's overwhelming amount of information has tilted the value toward quantity of reading, even if superficial. And our easy access to content makes it feels as if we no longer need to memorize it. We rely instead on noting its location; we dogear book pages, underline paragraphs, bookmark websites, and save videos. Our memory has become an index of knowledge; it shows us where to find what we are looking for, but never holds the knowledge itself.

While it's good to remember the location of knowledge, not memorizing the information itself limits our use of it. Imagine you read a book on first aid. You dogeared it, underlined the most important parts, and placed it back in your bookshelf for future reference. That's a great start, but if you need to give first aid to someone on the street, it's useless to know where to find the book on your bookshelf or which chapter to review.

Videos, books, and all other forms of external memory are a great advance of our race; they allow us to share and record information. We should take advantage of their increasing availability, but we must remember that learning and mastering a skill doesn't happen outside of us; it happens inside. We need to internalize knowledge to make the best out of it and be able to use it when we need it. How do we get better at memorizing, then? Let's look at some strategies.

THE STRATEGIES

Practice Retrieval

Practice retrieval is the technical name for testing. We know it in the form of quizzes, exams, drills, and flashcards. But testing can also be as simple as going through study material and self-questioning, writing the information down from memory, teaching it to someone else, or having our coach ask us questions. Essentially, anything that forces us to recall from memory is a form of practice retrieval.

Testing has two key benefits. The first one is stronger memories. The effort we put into recalling what we learned before strengthens the mental pathways associated with it. And the more effort we put into recall, the bigger the benefit (what Robert Bjork, a renowned expert in learning, calls "desirable difficulty"). For this reason, we should test straight from memory and avoid testing that provides multiple choice. As we discussed earlier, multiple choice relies on recognition over recall and doesn't provide an accurate assessment of what we can remember without cues.

The other benefit is feedback. Testing reveals what we know, what we don't, and what needs improvement. SWAT teams, firefighters, pilots, and people in other high-stakes fields use practice retrieval often—in the form of drills, tests, and simulations—to assess their knowledge and stay on top of it. It helps them differentiate between what they know for sure and what they think they know and then adjust their training accordingly. The same benefit applies to other skills, high-stakes or not. Testing gives us an assessment of our knowledge and skill, revealing where we need to put more attention.

Testing is one of the best learning strategies out there; we should use it as often as possible. It doesn't have to be something formal, though. We are testing to improve our learning, not to get a grade. We can use flashcards, put knowledge into our own words, create our own quizzes, or simply take time to remember information in our own mind. What's important is that we practice recalling. And remember, it's not about always answering right—it's about the effort behind trying. Even if we get answers wrong, we support our learning. On one side, by getting feedback we can make adjustments, and on the other, research shows that when we get the answers wrong, we become more receptive to learn the right ones after, a win for testing on all sides.

Spaced Repetition

Repetition strengthens the memory of what we study. And though it's not an efficient strategy for memorizing *new* knowledge, it's valuable for solidifying existing knowledge. We'll be using repetition in the form of tests and reviews following a spaced repetition model. This means expanding or contracting the time between tests and reviews depending on how well we remember the material.

Let's imagine we are going into cooking and want to memorize recipes—ingredients, steps, cooking times, and temperatures—to start building a *repertoire*. Here's how to test and review under spaced repetition.

We begin by studying the recipes. Then, we'll test our knowledge around thirty minutes after the study session. The test will show us which recipes we remember and which we don't.

For the ones we remember, we'll retest them the day after. If we still remember them, we'll retest a few days after that (then a week later, then a few weeks later). In essence, we extend the time between testing if every time we do it we can recall the recipes.

Now, if we can't remember a recipe, we'll review it after the test and then restart the spaced repetition timeline for it (test it in a day, then in a few days, then in a few weeks).

A shorthand for spaced repetition is that if we remember what we test—we recall the knowledge—we progressively increase the time between retesting. But if we don't remember, we need to review the material and restart the testing cycle.

Spacing out testing and reviews allows our knowledge to fade enough so that it's effortful to recall. And as mentioned earlier, it's the effort we put into it that strengthens our memories. We also need some forgetting to benefit from further reviews. If we revisit material too often, we become familiar with it and assume we've memorized it, even if we haven't.

Spaced repetition helps us with that calculated forgetting, making it ideal for solidifying *knowledge*.* And though the scheduling seems complex, there are flashcard apps and software with a built-in spaced repetition system (SRS) that can take care of it for us.† We only need to turn the knowledge we want to test into flashcards, which should be possible for almost anything, and the app will handle the time intervals.

Make Elaborate Memories

As we discussed in the memory principles, having multiple connections to a memory increases the quality of the encoding and later recall. Creating these connections is known as *elaboration*, and we'll use it to make information, techniques, or principles of our craft more memorable.

For a general example, we'll go back to remembering the name of someone we met. Hearing the name once is often not enough for a lasting memory—the information is not elaborate enough to stick. To make it memorable, we have to create associations between the name and the person. One option is connecting the name to a similar-sounding visual cue. If we meet a bearded man named Marc, we could associate his name with an "arc," which sounds similar, and then visualize Paris's *Arc de Triomphe* upside down as Marc's beard. This creates an elaborate memory that makes the name easier to remember.

---

* Remember: here, we are working on memorizing the knowledge parts of our craft—theory, concepts, steps, principles. We'll work on the procedural ones during practice (chapter 7).

† A good option is the free, open-source program "Anki."

The same principle applies to learning skills. We can elaborate on abstract information and make it memorable by associating it with things that sound or look alike and are easy to visualize. In learning basic chords on the guitar, for instance, we can associate the finger forms with visual images similar to them. "C" could be a stairway and "G" giving someone the finger. They look very similar.

The same would apply to learning yoga asanas. We can associate our body position with familiar shapes to better remember them. And in learning languages, we can associate new words with something in our language that sounds similar to it. For example, the French word "*marché*" (market) sounds similar to marching. So, we can imagine ourselves marching toward a supermarket to buy groceries. This visual association is easier to remember than the abstract sound "*marché*." Here, we are crossing into a form of elaboration known as mnemonics, the subject of our next strategy.

Mnemonics

The definition of mnemonics is memory aids or techniques. When we were making memories more elaborate by connecting them to other things, like associating the French word "*marché*" with the similar-sounding English word "marching," we were using mnemonics. But the term also refers to structured memory systems that follow specific rules for associating information with images that grab our attention and are easy to remember. Let's explore the two most used by memory champions: the *loci* system and the PAO (Person-Action-Object) system.

The Loci System (Aka Memory Palace or Journey Method)

The loci system is a powerful memory technique that takes advantage of two things our memory is strongest at: images and space.

The system works by associating imagery with physical spaces. We start by thinking of a location we know well or a path we are familiar with. This could be your house, your school, a park you like, or the street you live on (the requirement is that you know the spaces and fixed objects in this location well). Then, we connect what we want to memorize to those spaces and objects—which take on the name of "markers" or "loci."*

Let's use your home for an example. In it, you find "fixed" objects and spaces, such as the front door, the kitchen, and the furniture. We'll use these as the loci, and they will work as anchors for what you'll memorize. As for what to memorize, let's take tasks from a to-do list to keep things simple:

- Withdraw money from an ATM
- Call your best friend
- Take your car to the repair shop
- Buy bread
- Meditate

Now that we have the loci and the items to memorize, we'll create imagery connecting the two. Here are the basic guidelines for our visualizations:

---

* *Locus* (plural *loci*) is the Latin word for place. In the context of these memory techniques, it encompasses both spaces—rooms, roads, parks—and the fixed objects in them—windows, street signs, trees.

1. The images should be vivid, and the more details we imagine, the better.
2. The images should interact with us or with other objects.
3. The images or their interactions should be unusual. (This goes back to the principle that what's outstanding or unexpected catches our attention.)

To start, imagine you are in front of your home. As you open the front door, a wave of money pushes it open, and you have to fight your way through all this cash to get inside. This is your cue for "withdraw money from the ATM." Then, you walk into your bathroom and see your best friend washing a giant cell phone in the sink. That's the cue for "call your best friend." After that, you move into the living room to sit down to relax, but your car is sitting on the couch, taking all the space. He's watching a demolition derby in horror. That's your cue for "take the car to the repair shop." You then go into the kitchen to grab something to eat. You are surprised to find that your fridge is now a giant loaf of bread and has a bite mark on it. Someone must have been starving, your cue for "buy bread." Finally, you go into your bedroom and find your dog seated in the lotus position on your bed, surrounded by a colorful aura and about to reach enlightenment, the cue for "meditate."

I know this is bizarre, but that's the point. Our attention and memory are attracted to what's novel, outrageous, funny. It may also seem complicated, but the loci system is fast and easy once we get used to it. Better still, the memories we create are solid. They will last longer than if we memorized them through repetition. And when it comes to memorizing large amounts of information, the loci system is one of the best techniques to do it. See it for yourself: let time pass before doing a mental walk around your home again, a day or even a week, and you'll find these images still there waiting for you.

The loci system can be used to memorize almost anything. It's only a matter of creating visualizations for what we want to memorize and connecting them to physical objects and spaces in a location. In ancient Greece and Rome, orators used the system to memorize speeches. They attached images representing the main ideas of a speech to loci, and when it was time to speak, they would take a mental walk going from locus to locus, letting the images show them what to say next.

In our times, memory champions have used this method to memorize thousands of digits of pi or the entire *Oxford English Dictionary*. For our purpose of learning a craft, we can use it to memorize bits of knowledge or steps in a process, such as the ingredient list and cooking steps for making a dish if learning to cook, or pre-landing checks and procedures if learning to fly a plane.

I recommend you give the loci system a try. It's impressive how well our memory works when we feed it the input it's meant to process—images, space, emotions, and novelty. If you decide to try it, here are some guidelines to follow:

- Know the place or path and the fixed objects in it well. You don't want to struggle to remember what was in the location in the first place. Also, only use objects you know will remain in their position and are hard to overlook.
- Give objects room to be noticed. If you overcrowd a space with them, it will be more likely you'll skip some.
- Always go through the place or path in the same direction. Front to back, back to front, clockwise, or counterclockwise—any direction is fine as long as it's the same every

time. And go from object to object in the same order. This will help avoid overlooking things.
- Choose objects that are different from each other. If two chairs in your living room look similar, use only one as a locus; otherwise, it may get confusing.
- Create images that grab your attention and make an impression—active, funny, sexual, ridiculous, dramatic, out of the ordinary. Visualize details, and when possible, have the images interact with you as you walk around; it will make them easier to remember.
- If you want to store information *permanently* in a location, make sure you don't use it to memorize anything else. Also, revisit it once in a while, so the knowledge doesn't fade.
- If you are storing information *temporarily,* make sure you do a mental "sweep" of all the associations attached to the loci so they can be used again. This may sound strange, but going over them in your mind and mentally vanishing the previous connections will clear the space to start anew.

The PAO (Person-Action-Object) System

The Person-Action-Object system works as a pre-set of mental images we can assign to bits of information to make them easier to remember.* The technique is used for things we repeatedly need to memorize in a changing order. In memory championships, for instance, competitors use it to memorize a random series of numbers or playing cards. The PAO system gives that information, which is hard to visualize and

---

* The system is made of a combination of several methods and contributions from different people over the years, so no specific attribution is given.

memorize, a set of images that better stick to our memory, all while keeping the information in order.

Let's look at an example. We'll use the system to memorize playing cards, a skill that could get you banned from casinos and hated by your Blackjack gambling friends.

In this instance, the PAO system consists of assigning an image of a person (P) doing an action (A) on an object (O)* to each of the fifty-two cards in a deck. It can be any person, any action, and any object as long as it is memorable and easy to differentiate from the ones you assign to other cards. For example, the ten of diamonds could be the boxing legend Muhammad Ali punching a boxing bag, the seven of spades the scientist Carl Sagan launching the Voyager probe, and the jack of clubs the philosopher Friedrich Nietzsche hugging a horse.

Once we have an image for each card (a person acting on an object), we can combine them to memorize three cards in a row. If we want to remember the sequence seven of spades, jack of clubs, and ten of diamonds (7S, JC, 10D), for example, we take the person we assigned to the 7S, Carl Sagan, performing the action we gave to the JC, hugging, on the object we associated with 10D, a boxing bag. The image for the three cards in that order (7S, JC, 10D) becomes Carl Sagan hugging a boxing bag.

If the sequence were instead jack of clubs, ten of diamonds, and seven of spades (JC, 10D, 7S), we would take the person for JC, Nietzsche, then add the action for 10D, punching, and the object for 7S, the Voyager probe. This time we end up with Nietzsche punching the Voyager probe.

Let's do one more. We'll take the sequence ten of dia-

---

* The category "objects" can also include animals or plants.

monds, seven of spades, and jack of clubs (10D, 7S, JC). Here, we'll visualize the person for 10D, Muhammad Ali, doing the action for 7S, launching, on the object for JC, a horse. Now we have Muhammad Ali launching a horse.

Since we assign a person, an action, and an object to every card in a deck, we can memorize sets of three with a single image or "story" like we did above. In doing so, we are "chunking" three pieces of information into one. In our example, we'd have either Carl Sagan hugging a boxing bag for 7S, JC, 10D, Nietzsche punching the Voyager probe for JC, 10D, 7S, or Muhammad Ali launching a horse for 10D, 7S, JC.

If we wanted to memorize longer sequences, we could combine those "chunks." Let's say we want to memorize the following card sequence: seven of spades, jack of clubs, ten of diamonds, jack of clubs, ten of diamonds, seven of spades, ten of diamonds, seven of spades, and jack of clubs (7S, JC, 10D, JC, 10D, 7S, 10D, 7S, JC). *Note: we are repeating the same cards in a different order to keep things simple, but in practice it works the same way with different cards in any sequence.*

We've already created an image for all of them: The first three cards (7S, JC, 10D) are Carl Sagan hugging a boxing bag. The next three (JC, 10D, and 7S) are Nietzsche punching the Voyager probe. And the last three (10D, 7S, and JC) are Muhammad Ali launching a horse. We have three images, then, one for each set of three cards. Let's now leverage on our ability to remember narratives and create a story between them.

One day Carl Sagan was hugging a boxing bag. This made Nietzsche jealous; he also wanted to hug it. Out of rage, Nietzsche started punching the Voyager probe. Muhammad Ali, worried they would start a fight, tried to distract both men by doing something outrageous, launching a horse in the air. All three men looked up to the sky as the horse flew away.

There we have it: 7S, JC, 10D, JC, 10D, 7S, 10D, 7S, JC.

Another way to connect the three images is by using the PAO system in combination with the loci system we saw earlier. We'll take the same location as before, your home, and the same loci: the front door, bathroom sink, and living room sofa (we won't need the others). Let's now attach each image—Carl Sagan hugging a boxing bag, Nietzsche punching the Voyager probe, and Muhammad Ali launching a horse—to those loci:

You get home and find that your front door is blocked by Carl Sagan hugging a boxing bag. You have to go around him to enter your place. Next, you walk past the bathroom and see Nietzsche punching the Voyager probe to pieces. He's standing on the sink so he can start from the top and work his way down. Finally, you move into the living room and see Muhammad Ali ready to launch a horse into space; he's using your couch as a launch platform. 7S, JC, 10D, JC, 10D, 7S, 10D, 7S, JC.

The PAO system is a powerful memory tool. Though we used it here to memorize playing cards, it can have applications across domains. In music, for instance, it can be used to memorize chord progressions. Musicians use the same chords all the time; it's the order that changes depending on the song. So, just as Carl Sagan hugging a boxing bag was the seven of spades, jack of clubs, and ten of diamonds (7S, JC, 10D) for a card player, it could be Em–D–G for a musician. And the same can be done for dance moves in choreography, football plays in a game, or anything that involves an inventory of recurrent "parts" we need to memorize in different orders.

The downside of the PAO system is that it takes time to set up. We have to assign and memorize a person, action, and object for each piece of information—each chord, dance move, football play, or card in a deck—but once the system is set up, it makes memorizing sequences fast and easy.

Memorizing is a crucial part of learning any skill. We need to internalize theory, concepts, and steps so we can take them into practice. Here, we conclude the first phase of the process, "learning what to do." Now, we must transform our knowledge into abilities. We'll shift our attention to "learning *how* to do it," and it all begins with *practice*.

CHAPTER 7

Practice

To practice with vigor is to be near to magnanimity.
—CONFUCIUS

So far in our model, we've focused on understanding and memorizing theory, concepts, and steps—acquiring knowledge. But that doesn't translate into abilities. Reading books on painting and art theory, for example, will teach us about the craft but won't develop our painting skills. For that, we need to practice.

Another important distinction between knowledge and abilities is that the cognitive side of a craft can be transferred through books, videos, or seminars, and we can learn it within weeks or months. But the procedural one can't be transferred; we have to develop it ourselves, and it may take years to do so. This can make it feel more gratifying to focus on learning theory than putting in the practice. We move more quickly through books and videos—and get a sense of accomplishment from having finished them—than we improve abilities through action.

Practice is hard work and improvement slow, too slow to

give us the immediate gratification and illusion of progress we get from focusing on the knowledge side of our craft. But without it, we can't develop our skills. We can't read or watch our way to mastery; we must practice. It's the essence of learning any craft, and despite some people's negative feelings toward it, it can be the most exciting and rewarding part of learning. So, what makes good practice? And how can we maximize the results we get from the time and effort we put into it? That will be the subject of this chapter.

THE PRINCIPLES

Practice vs. Repetition

We have two goals in practice: increase our current level and solidify what we already learned. Repetition helps us with the latter, solidifying our abilities, but it's not a way to expand them. Think of how long you've been brushing your teeth or walking. That's years of repetition without getting better. At some point, you felt proficient enough and stopped trying to improve. All the repetition you've done since then only reinforced the way you brush your teeth and walk, not improved it.

Repetition can be good or bad, depending on what we repeat. The process does not discriminate between right or wrong. Think now of people who've been driving for years and are still terrible at it. Repetition didn't make them better drivers; it only solidified their driving style, with all its mistakes and bad habits. The main role of repetition is reinforcement, so, for it to be useful, we need to repeat the right things. That means building our abilities correctly in the first place. For that, we turn to a different process, deliberate practice.

Deliberate Practice

This is the ideal form of practice. The term and concept were introduced by the renowned expert in expertise K. Anders Ericsson. In his words, deliberate practice is "purposeful practice that knows where it is going and how to get there." Let's look at key elements to satisfy those conditions.

Deliberate practice has well-defined goals for the practice session. Practice should always have an aim, and it can't be as vague as "to get better." We need to know exactly what we want to work on and then design a session for it. The goal could be to improve a specific part of the skill, fix a mistake or bad habit, or refine a difficult technique. What's important is to know what we want to achieve and then go after it. (It's not enough to simply show up.) As an added benefit, having clear goals makes progress easier to track and notice, helping us stay motivated.

Deliberate practice needs to be deliberate. We have to give practice our undivided attention, not just our time. If our mind is wandering and we are cruising through a practice session, we'll fall into mindless repetition. Deliberate practice demands all our energy; it's exhausting, but the payoff is worth it. One hour of deliberate practice will yield more results than several hours of mindless practice. Think quality over quantity.

Deliberate practice stands on proven training techniques. Improving fast depends to a great extent on the degree to which our chosen craft is developed. Each generation stands on the shoulders of the one before. If we are in a new field, there will be few experts and little consensus on the best approach to learn and master it. But for fields such as music, where there's been countless masters and hundreds of years of collective wisdom, we'll find well-established guidelines to study and practice the art. In that sense, part of how much we can optimize our practice depends on the availability of proven guidelines to follow.

Deliberate practice requires guidance. Closely related to following proven training techniques is having a coach or teacher to guide us through the process—someone who can show us the way, teach us those proven training techniques, and challenge us to be better. The value of a good mentor can't be overstated; they play a key role in developing our skills. (We'll discuss mentors in depth in chapter 13.)

Deliberate practice builds on good feedback. Feedback is a key element of improvement. It shows us what we are doing right and what we are doing wrong. Without it, mistakes would go unnoticed, and we wouldn't know what to improve. We'll be dedicating a chapter to this important subject (chapter 10). There, we'll cover what makes good feedback, ways to get it, and how to make the most out of it.

Deliberate practice happens on the sweet spot. Practice is most effective when we do it at the edge of our capabilities, where we reach outside our comfort zone. This is often called "the sweet spot," a point where our abilities are challenged enough to keep us engaged but not too much that it overwhelms us. The renowned psychologist and author of *Flow: The Psychology of Optimal Experience*, Mihaly Csikszentmihalyi, calls it the right ratio of the difficulty of the task over our ability to perform it (challenge/skill ratio). If what we are doing is too easy, we disengage from it and fall into repetition mode. But if it's too hard, we get frustrated, start to break good technique, and lose control trying to keep up.

How much should we challenge ourselves to reach the sweet spot? Dr. Csikszentmihalyi writes that the general thinking is to stretch our capabilities by about 4 percent. That's difficult to imagine, but the point he wants to make is that it doesn't take much. For a more practical standard, we'll refer again to Dr. Ericsson. He describes the sweet spot as the place where we get things right between 50 percent and 80 percent of the time.

Practicing on the sweet spot is a struggle, and not always enjoyable. In fact, Dr. Ericsson considers struggle the defining emotion of deep practice. And while training under these conditions can be engaging, gratifying, and even addictive, top performers rarely describe it as fun. "I love to write," Ernest Hemingway said, "but it has never gotten any easier to do and you can't expect it to if you keep trying for something better than you can do."

As a guideline, if we feel absent-minded, at ease, or mostly having fun during a practice session, it's likely we are not on the sweet spot. That said, effortful practice doesn't mean dreadful. Challenges are enjoyable, but they are still challenges. Think of video games. We get bored if they are too easy. The joy of playing them comes from being challenged and having to get better because of it.

Challenging ourselves is desirable, but we must be careful not to push too hard too soon. Pressure disrupts learning and makes it inflexible. The literal and metaphorical idea of throwing someone in the water so they learn to swim creates a traumatic experience that can affect future learning. So, even though some people will learn to swim after being thrown in the water, such a shocking experience can make it harder for them to learn proper technique later and even discourage them from taking on swimming as a sport. The ideal way to develop our abilities is through small progressive stretches, not by overwhelming our system—and this is especially important in developing physical skills, where pushing too hard too soon can get us injured.

Massed vs. Distributed Practice

While deliberate practice centers on how to practice, we also need to consider how often and for how long to do it, the frequency and length of practice sessions. There are two approaches: massed practice and distributed practice (also known as cramming and spaced practice, respectively).

Cramming is when we try to pack long hours of practice or study into a few sessions. Distributed practice, on the other hand, is when we space out our practice sessions over longer periods of time.

Let's say we have eight hours a week to practice. If we put them all in one day and don't do anything else for the rest of the week, we are cramming. But if we distribute those eight hours into four two-hour practice sessions throughout the week, we are doing distributed practice.

Research on learning has made it clear: distributed practice is a better strategy for long-lasting learning. It's more effective to practice for one hour, five times a week, than to cram five hours of practice into a single day once a week. Similarly, practicing three days a week for a month is better than doing it for twelve days straight and not practicing again until the following month.

Cramming *feels* like rapid learning, but it's because we are exposed to the material for long hours. In reality, only a small percentage of it is internalized. If we were to spend the same amount of time on either distributed practice or cramming, distributed practice would yield better results.

Studies looking to measure the effectiveness of the two approaches shows that when students are tested soon after cramming (hours or a day later), they score higher than those adhering to a spaced practice routine. But the boost doesn't last long. When the same students are tested days or weeks later, the "spaced practice" students remember more than those who cram.

Spaced practice has better long-term benefits because it offers an advantage cramming cannot: balance. We need enough time between practice sessions to process what we learn and consolidate new memories, but it can't be so long that we lose our progress. Distributed practice follows this principle: manageable practice sessions followed by moderate breaks. Cramming, on the contrary, gives us too much to process at once. And if our cramming sessions are few and far between, we lose most of our "progress" from one session to the next.

Another form of balance we get with spaced practice is moderate forgetting. We want some of our learning to fade, though not too much—as can happen with distant cramming sessions. Moderate forgetting supports learning in two ways. First, it shows us which parts didn't have strong encoding in the first place and need more attention. And second, the effort we put into trying to recall what we studied reinforces the memory of it once reviewed—or remembered. If this sounds familiar to our "practice retrieval" discussion in the previous chapter, it should. Spaced practice is a form of practice retrieval. By allowing time between practice sessions, our next one works as a test, forcing us to recall what we've learned before.

Let's take a practical example. Imagine you are learning *Surya Namaskar*, the sun salutation in yoga. After an hour of practice, you can remember the poses and how to transition into them. Instead of practicing for another hour when it's still fresh, it's better to wait until later in the day or the next day. You will forget some of it, but it'll work in your favor. The effort you put into remembering the poses and transitions will reinforce the learning. Yes, it feels harder to learn this way, but it makes for strong learning that lasts.

The question then becomes: how much time should we allow before practicing or studying the same thing? It depends. It's different for different people, different skills, and different levels of difficulty. There is no fixed rule, but here's the principle to follow: leave enough time so it feels effortful to remember but not so long that you forget most of it and have to relearn it.

This doesn't mean you shouldn't practice your craft every day, or even twice a day if you want to; just vary what you practice to allow time between practicing *the same thing*. You can even do this within a practice session. If you plan to practice for four hours one day, for example, you could practice one thing the first hour and again in the final hour instead of doing it for two hours straight. (More on this in the "Interleaved Practice" section under "The Strategies.")

Though we just declared distributed practice a better learning strategy than cramming, we were referring to cramming as an intense *but* inconsistent approach—long practice or study sessions every now and then. The only benefit that comes from this is a short-term boost in performance, with minimal long-term impact. But under certain conditions, cramming can be useful.

A valuable form of cramming is immersion (*sustained cramming*). This is an intense *and* consistent approach: long practice or study sessions frequently over several weeks or months. *Sustained cramming* triggers plastic changes in the brain, the conditions we are looking for in learning. In other words, it works.

A great example of learning through immersion comes from Tim Ferriss, an avid—and successful—learner, and the author of several productivity and self-improvement bestsellers. In his book *The 4-Hour Chef*, which Ferriss describes as an accelerated learning book disguised as a cookbook, he explains his approach to learning cooking skills in a short time. Ferriss immersed himself in the subject. For weeks, everything he read and watched was related to cooking, and more to our discussion, he crammed most of his learning.

When writing about cramming and its criticism, Ferriss argued, "CRAMMING isn't pass–fail. Let's say you attempt culinary cram school—cramming six months into 48 hours, as I did. Let's then say that you retain only 40% of what was taught. If you develop the motor patterns to continue practicing *correctly*, which is exactly what happened to me, did you fail? Of course not! Even 40% of six months means that you absorbed 2.4 months of skills in 48 hours." A key phrase in Ferriss's statement is "to continue practicing *correctly*." He never claimed that the forty-eight-hour cram was enough to learn the art of cooking, but that it was an excellent way to jumpstart the learning process.

If you want to cram or enjoy doing it, the way to get the most out of it is to counter the low retention rate by either sustaining the cramming and turning it into immersion—like Ferriss did to learn cooking skills—or following it up with consistent spaced practice. What you shouldn't do is cram one day and not practice or review again for days or weeks. You'll lose most of your progress between sessions.

Another good approach to cramming is to use it during two learning steps unrelated to practice, *exploring* and *understanding*. This is when we are getting an overview of our craft, gathering a lot of information, and making sense of concepts, but not yet concerned with memorizing or practicing. Cramming is a good strategy here because we get to explore and process large amounts of knowledge in short periods of time.

When I take on a new skill, I research it for days, cramming as much information as I can. It's my way of exploring and understanding the pieces involved. During this time, I'm not expecting to retain what I study. What I'm after is gathering knowledge, seeing the big picture, and getting a better idea of what awaits me. Cramming at this stage gets me into a flow of discovery that deepens my interest in the skill in ways periodic engagement wouldn't.

Different Practice for Different Skills

In *The Talent Code* and *The Little Book of Talent,* Daniel Coyle points out that there are two types of skills or sub-skills: *flexible* and *precise*. Certain crafts are composed of both, while others are dominated by one. And depending on the type, we need to adjust our practice. Let's explore both types and how to approach them.

Precise skills need to be executed the same way every time, a precise process to the desired result. Classical music interpretation is an example. Musicians practice to play an exact note at an exact time, every time. The music piece doesn't change—it's precise—so their goal is to replicate it time and again.

Flexible skills, on the other hand, can be executed in different ways to get the desired result. The process is flexible. Consider chess, for example. Every game is different, and players can't rely on the same moves to win them all. They need to be flexible and adapt to the circumstances, changing their moves and tactics as the match progresses. There's no one way to play chess. There are only sets of rules, principles, and guidelines; it's up to each player to decide how to use them.

In some cases, a craft can be flexible or precise, depending on how we intend to use it. In music, for instance, classical interpretation is precise, as explained above, but jazz improvisation is flexible. The goal of jazz improvisation is to express a mood, feeling, or theme, not to play the same notes in the same order every time—that would be the opposite of improvisation. When improvising, a jazz player is flexible with notes and melody, using them in different ways and following only the principles and good qualities of the style, instead of a predefined composition.

Comedy is another example of a craft that can be flexible or precise. Scripted comedians practice a set over and over until refined and memorized. Then, every show, they perform it as close as possible to the ideal version. On the other side, improvisational comedians don't follow a script. Every night they go on stage, they have to adapt to a different storyline that builds on itself; this requires flexibility.

There is no more merit to one or the other; both scripted comedy and improv are hard to perform. The point is that they involve different kinds of practice. Scripted comedians spend long hours drilling their set so they can replicate it night after night—that's precision. The improv comedians work on learning to use the principles of comedy in an always-changing array of stories and scenarios—that's flexibility.*

Since flexible skills have multiple paths to the desired result, we must learn to navigate different scenarios. This requires building *diverse* experience to internalize underlying

---

* I used scripted comedians for a *precise skill* example, but within their work are things that fall into *flexible skills*. When comedians are creating their set in the first place, they are not following an exact path. They are using their knowledge of comedy and their idea of a theme to put concepts and material together to build it. Writing comedy, then, falls under flexible skills. But once the set is written and the comedian wants a tight, replicable set to perform night after night, they switch to a precise part of their craft.

principles and patterns. In chess, players need to play and study many games to develop their skill. It's how they form a base of moves, strategies, and structures they can use as points of reference and guidelines for playing future matches. Again, diversity of experience is key here. We wouldn't expect a chess player to get any better repeating the same game for weeks.

As for precise skills, doing the same thing over and over is not only expected—it's desired. The goal is to refine an exact process that leads to a desired result. This requires building *specific* experience. For classical music interpreters, it means practicing the same piece over and over until it's right. The notes, chords, or melodies of the piece are always the same, so the focus is on playing them as precisely as possible. Again, specific experience is key here. A classical music interpreter can't jump from one piece to another, never practicing each more than once, and expect to sound great at any of them.

A simplified way to think about flexible and precise skills is that in flexible skills, there are many roads to achieve our goal (the process can vary), while in precise skills, there's only one (the process is not meant to change). The focus of practice for flexible skills, then, is on internalizing principles and patterns and learning to apply them in different ways—developing flexibility. And for precise skills, the focus is on executing the same moves, in the same way, every time—developing precision.

Flexible skills can be frustrating for people who want certainty and fail-proof methods to everything they do. By their nature, those skills don't have a "right answer," and it's this need for flexibility that makes them thrilling for those who pursue them. On the other side, precise skills can frustrate those wanting variety in the process. Such precision demands sticking to defined moves and practicing them repeatedly until they are "right." For some of us, having a clear sense of what we need to do and progressively moving toward it—such as getting better at playing a song we love—is very gratifying.

This is not to say that you should choose one skill over another based on your personality. You should be in the craft you are passionate about but be prepared to put in the type of practice it requires.

THE STRATEGIES

Embrace Practice

Learning a skill takes practice, hours upon hours of practice. We can use strategies to optimize it, but there are no shortcuts. We'll still have to practice—everyone does.

For the few hours we see a musician on stage or a great athlete on the field, there are countless hours of training to make that happen. In that sense, if we want to play the piano, we must be ready to practice the piano. The dream of performing our favorite piece will never happen if we are not willing to go through the hours of work it takes to learn the instrument. As Hemingway once wrote, "There are some things which cannot be learned quickly, and time, which is all we have, must be paid heavily for their acquiring."

Our first strategy, then, is to embrace practice. Without a commitment to doing the work and even learning to take pleasure from it, we won't get far. Practice is the essence of learning and mastering any skill. There's no way around it.

Deconstruct, Isolate, Chunk, Reconstruct

Every skill is composed of different parts. It would be overwhelming and counterproductive to try to learn all of them at the same time. The right approach is to deconstruct the skill into smaller parts first and practice those in isolation. Then, as we get better, chunk the parts back together until we reconstruct the whole.

Think of how we learned to write. Starting out, we studied individual letters. Then we put them together to form words, then put words together to form sentences, and so on. We started from the simplest form and added complexity as we got better. This progression is the basis for learning any skill. It sounds obvious, but we often forget that learning builds on itself. We are meant to start small and add to it, instead of trying to do all at once.

A great example of learning from simple to complex comes from one of the best books on learning I've come across, *The Art of Learning: An Inner Journey to Optimal Performance* by international chess master and martial arts champion, Josh Waitzkin. In the book, he explains his approach to learning chess. Instead of learning the game starting with a full board and working on openings, he worked on endgame with few pieces on the board. Dealing with a small number of pieces—and thus fewer variables—allowed him to focus on smaller parts of chess and add complexity as he got better.

In Waitzkin's words, this approach also helped him to "touch high-level principles such as the power of empty space, tempo, or structural planning." Starting with low complexity gave him insights into the governing principles of the game—what Waitzkin calls "learning the macro from the micro."

It might seem counterintuitive to learn chess starting with endgame—for many, it's a backward approach—but it makes sense once we realize we are reducing complexity. When teaching children to swim, for instance, we don't start them with all the variables. Instead, we deconstruct the skill for them in two parts: kicking movement and arms movement. We make them work on one part in isolation first and then add the other.

The "deconstruct, isolate, chunk, reconstruct" process is not only for learning a skill in the first place but also for improving it. Even the great swimmer Michael Phelps would do practice drills using just his arms or legs. It's hard to know which parts of your technique can be improved if you are doing everything at once. By deconstructing a style and isolating parts of it in his practice, Phelps could find what was holding him back and work on it. Once improved, he could then chunk the pieces back together and reconstruct the whole technique now better than before.

Focus on Fundamentals

Aside from exploring *how* to practice, we also need to discuss *what* to practice. Even if we follow effective practice principles, we'll waste time and effort if we are learning the "wrong" things. Tim Ferriss put it best: "Material beats method." What we study can make a bigger difference than how we study it. Ideally, we want to have both on point, but his lesson is that effective learning doesn't lie in the process alone but also in the content we put through it.

So, what should we practice? "Learn the fundamentals of the game and stick to them," says golf great Jack Nicklaus. Our focus must be on the fundamental parts of our craft: the moves, knowledge, and techniques that are most frequently used and that make the strongest impact. These parts form the base for everything else and are essential for mastering the skill.

Betty Edwards, author of one of the most respected books on drawing, *Drawing on the Right Side of the Brain,* makes a clear point about fundamentals, "All drawing is the same, broadly speaking, always involving the same ways of seeing and the same skills, the basic components of drawing. You might use different mediums, different papers, large or small formats, but for drawing still-life setups, the figure, random objects, portrait drawings, and even imaginary subjects or drawing from memory, it is all the same task, always requiring the same basic component skills."*

Edwards adds that in learning how to draw, our focus should be on the fundamental skills of drawing and not on subject matter such as "landscape drawing" or "figure drawing" or on drawing mediums, such as charcoal, pen and ink, or mixtures. She is telling us not to get lost in details and minor differences, but to work on the fundamental parts and develop an understanding of the principles of our craft before we move into specifics and specialties.

So, how do we identify the fundamentals of our craft? Instead of trying to figure them out on our own, we'll ask teachers, coaches, or advanced practitioners. They can help us deconstruct the skill into smaller parts or sub-skills and separate the essence from the optional.

Depending on the skill, we may need to take an extra step and identify the component parts of those fundamentals: *form* and *sequence.* Tim Ferriss makes the distinction between the two concepts in his book *The 4-Hour Chef.* In his words,

---

* According to Edwards, most of those component skills are "seeing skills": how to perceive edges, spaces, relationships, lights and shadows, and the gestalt.

"Form refers to things like grip, stance, and balance. Sequence refers to the order the parts move in."

In powerlifting, for instance, *form* has to do with the way lifters hold the bar, the position of their hands, the distance between their feet, and the alignment of their back. And sequence has to do with what moves first, second, and so on. For a *power clean*, a move where you lift a barbell from the floor to your shoulders, you start the force from your legs and hips to create momentum. Then, you shrug your shoulders and bring your elbows under the bar. You need to follow that sequence so you can generate the power and flow to complete the move.

Both form and sequence are important. In this powerlifting example, having poor form and/or poor sequence will hinder the lifter's force, kill momentum, and even put the athlete at risk of injury. Powerlifters need to give attention to both components, so they don't end up obsessing over one when it's the other that's holding them back. Or, as Ferriss puts it, "A lot of times, people will think they have poor form, when, in fact, it's their sequencing that's off." And though form and sequence don't play a key role in every skill or subskill, for those where it does—as we see in powerlifting—it's crucial to pay attention to them.

As a final note on fundamentals, there will be parts or sub-skills in our craft that are not essential for everyone but are important to us individually. These depend on our preferences, what we like or how we are planning to use our skills. When I was learning to play guitar, I only liked heavy metal and didn't want to play anything different. While I had to learn the fundamentals of the guitar, as any other guitar player would, there were other techniques I needed specifically for metal. Two examples are palm muting (muting open string strokes with your right palm) and power chords (chords played on the top two or three strings).

These techniques are not fundamental to music or guitar in general, but they were an essential part of the skill for me. Without them, I could not play the music I liked. So, aside from spending long hours working on the foundation of guitar playing, I also dedicated time to the techniques necessary for my preferred music style. The same will apply to any craft you are learning. Focus your practice on fundamentals, but also make sure to add what you like most or what fits your needs.

First Things (and Relevant Things) First

As important as *what* to practice is the order in which to practice it. We must work on our skills progressively and avoid jumping to advanced techniques if we haven't learned the basics. It's the idea of learning to walk before learning to run. First things come first.

We should also prioritize what we need now, instead of what we may need in the future. We are often tempted to learn fancy moves, techniques, or advanced principles we won't be using soon, and it ends up being a distraction. It's what scholars call "Just in Case" learning, though it can also be just-for-fun, just-for-ego, or just-for-curiosity learning.

While it's good to have an overview of everything involved in our craft, we must aim for what's been called "just-in-time learning," or learning things as we need them.* We make the most progress when we practice what matters now, what we can use now, and what we need now, at our current level.

---

* This is a concept derived from Toyota's famous Just-in-Time (JIT) manufacturing process.

Keep Practice Focused and Conscious

It's easy to let practice fall into autopilot, to just go through the moves or simply "show up," especially when we've been practicing for some time. But there's little value in this mindless practice. If we want to get better, our practice needs to be both focused and conscious.

Focused means that we keep our mind on the task at hand and avoid distractions, while *conscious* is knowing what we are doing and why we are doing it. As Leopold Auer, the renowned violinist, composer, conductor, and violin teacher, said, "Practice with your fingers and you need all day. Practice with your mind and you will do as much in 1 ½ hours." A belief echoed by Yo-Yo Ma: "Practicing is about quality, not quantity," said the great cellist when asked about his daily practice routine. "Some days I practice for hours; other days it will be just a few minutes."

So how do we stay focused and conscious during practice? To start, we must ask ourselves, "Am I thinking about being done or about doing it right?" Finishing an exercise, a drill, or punching the clock is not enough; we must strive to improve. Natalie Goldberg, author of *Writing Down the Bones*, put it best when she advised aspiring writers: "Don't just put in your time. That is not enough. You have to make great effort...Some people hear the rule 'Write every day' and do it and don't improve. They are just being dutiful."

Aside from self-awareness, the best way to stay focused and conscious is by making practice challenging—to push our capabilities and demand more of ourselves. When we reach out of our comfort zone, our mind naturally focuses on the task at hand. An everyday example is driving. If you've been driving for years, you no longer think about it. It's not challenging anymore, so you do it on "autopilot." But if you were forced to drive at a much higher speed than usual, you'd become very conscious and very focused, very fast. The same principle applies to everything else. Challenge forces our mind to engage.

Interleaved Practice

Interleaved practice, also known as varied practice, consists of mixing up the tasks or drills during a practice session instead of working on a single one. Let's use baseball as an example. If we are working on our batting skills, interleaving our practice means alternating between fastballs, breaking balls, and changeups in random order instead of working on a single pitch type for long blocks of time. By interleaving the pitches, we are putting emphasis on developing the fundamentals of being a good batter: a sense of distances, speeds, hand-eye coordination, and the ability to recognize a pitch and decide how to respond to it. Improving these fundamentals will make us better batters in the long term than proficiency in batting a single pitch type.

It's important to note that even though we are varying the practice, we are staying within one subject: batting. The goal in interleaved practice is to include variation within what we are working on, not to jump between unrelated things. In our example, we are not practicing batting for a few minutes and then working on our running, catching, or something else. We are only varying the pitches; the focus is still on batting.

How much should we interleave our practice? There's no rule. It depends on our craft, what we are practicing, and its complexity. What we can do is follow a guideline: do it enough that it feels challenging, but not so much that it gets overwhelming. For our batting example, we could begin practicing two basic pitches and alternating them at random. Then, we can add more as we improve, though never adding too much at a time that we get frustrated and break proper technique trying to keep up or that it makes us give up and walk away.

Interleaved practice feels slower and more challenging than working on the same drill for hours at a time, known as blocked practice or non-varied practice, but it results in stronger learning. We can think of interleaved practice as a form of spaced practice within a session. The variation we are adding with interleaved practice allows time between practicing the same thing, making it effortful again when we come back to it. It's the same benefit we get from spaced practice but on a smaller scale.

Aside from making practice more effortful, varying our practice also develops underlying abilities we need for our craft in general, not just for one piece of it. This is especially important for flexible skills where we need to analyze patterns and adapt to them. Back to our baseball example, we want the ability to adapt and be proficient at different pitches, not just one.

But interleaved practice can also be used for precise skills. If we are learning to play the piano, for instance, instead of working for hours on one scale, we can alternate between a few of them within a practice session. The same applies to chords. We can choose three or four and change from one to another in a different order. This will improve the underlying abilities we need to be better at playing chords, such as improved finger independence and sense of positioning on the keyboard. If working on a music piece instead, we can choose a few sections and alternate between them. We can practice one section for some time, move to another, then back to the first one. Note that we are staying within the same music piece; we are just alternating the time dedicated to each section.

Solo Practice

Solo practice is one of the best things we can do for our progress. As Pablo Picasso said, "Nothing can be accomplished without solitude." In the studies carried out by Dr. Ericsson on developing expert performance, all the students involved agreed that the most important factor for improvement was a solitary practice. Practicing alone develops discipline and focus; it also helps us find the sweet spot, the place at the edge of our abilities.

World-class performers from all fields spend long hours practicing alone, even those in team sports. In basketball, for instance, Michael Jordan and Kobe Bryant would arrive early for team practice so they could work on parts of their game on their own. Another example is chess. We think of it as a two-person game, but dedicated players spend hours alone studying games from the past—their own and those of masters. This solo study of the game is a key component of becoming a top chess player.

Regardless of the nature of our craft, whether a team sport or an individual field, we must look for ways to practice, or at least study, in solitude. Few strategies can match the impact of alone time in our skill.

Practice Partners

While spending solitary time immersed in our craft is crucial, practicing with others also has its benefits. Practice partners give us insight into our own level, our strengths, and our weaknesses. MMA fighting legend Frank Shamrock says we need what he calls the "plus, minus, equal"—someone better than us we can learn from (plus), someone lesser we can teach (minus), and someone equal to challenge ourselves (equal).

Each of them helps us in different ways. Those above our level can teach us how to get better. It's a model that's been successful throughout history. Experienced practitioners are paired with those on the intermediate and beginner levels to show them the ropes and help them improve. On the other side, with those below our level, we become the teachers—which has its learning benefits too. Teaching forces us to understand our subject better and to organize it so we can pass on the knowledge. At the same time, teaching works as practice recall and review, reinforcing the knowledge we already have. Finally, those at our same level make us stretch our ability through healthy competition and mutual challenge and encouragement, benefits that are not as present when training with someone far above or below.

Mental Practice

As the name suggests, mental practice happens in our mind. It consists of vividly imagining ourselves practicing the skill. This may sound like New Age nonsense, but there's solid research supporting it. Through brain imaging experiments, we know that our brain reacts to what's vividly imagined in similar ways to what's real. More related to our discussion, our brain recruits the same areas when we imagine moving parts of our body than when we move them in real life. So, if we imagine practicing our craft, we'll use—and strengthen—the same cognitive pathways we would in real practice.

In the words of Yo-Yo Ma, "Practicing is not only playing your instrument, either by yourself or rehearsing with others—it also includes imagining yourself practicing. Your brain forms the same neural connections and muscle memory whether you are imagining the task or actually doing it." And while mental practice is not meant to replace physical practice, research shows that it provides many of its benefits; in other words, it's the next best thing.

Artists and athletes of different fields use mental practice to train and prepare for performance. Dancers, for instance, mentally go through their routines before going on stage, and racers mentally go around a track, practicing their shifting, braking, and acceleration before race day.

The gymnast champion and Olympian Simone Biles talks about this concept as dream routines, "You stand on the side and you kind of dream your routine in your head so that you get a feel of what you're about to do going up to that equipment." She then adds, "I go through every skill on my head, exactly what I'm going to do so that I can perform it to the best of my ability once I hit whatever equipment I'm on."

A note to keep in mind for getting the most out of mental practice is to be fully involved in it. We must visualize ourselves doing the practice and "being there" as with as much detail as possible—as if we were doing it in real life. Also, the benefits of mental practice increase when followed by real practice, so use it in combination with the real thing, not as a substitute.

Plan the Practice

We need to plan our practice to get the most out of it. Knowing in advance what we want to work on and how we are going to do it will help us maximize our efforts. Let's look at key points for planning our practice sessions.

Purpose. Practice is not about showing up, going through the moves, or putting in the time; it's about making progress. As legendary boxer Muhammad Ali advised, "Don't count the days, make the days count." And to make progress, we need clear objectives. It doesn't have to be a detailed plan, but we have to go into each practice session knowing what specific part of our skill we want to work on. Having an objective in mind will make it easier to choose drills and exercises to reach it.

Few things at a time. Related to having clear objectives for our practice sessions is working on a few things at a time. It's tempting to practice many parts of our craft in one day, but learning requires focus, effort, and time; if we try to do too much at once, none of it will get the attention it needs. We should choose between one to three things to practice in any given session. Remember: there will be a time for everything, just not everything at the same time.

Checklists. Checklists are a way to remind ourselves of important points to pay attention to during practice. For someone going into bodybuilding, a checklist for squat "practice" (workout) may include: keep back straight, gaze forward, control the move, keep knees in line with feet. For someone learning tennis, the checklist would be related to the way to hold the racket, the position on the court, and the ideal height at which to hit the ball. When we have checklists, we get to refer back to them during practice and make sure we are not leaving important things out.

Length and Breaks. Deliberate practice is exhausting; if we don't give ourselves breaks, we'll burn out and have diminishing returns. Ideally, we should take between five- and twenty-minute breaks for every forty to fifty-five minutes of intense practice, and do no more than a four- to five-hour session in a day, practice and breaks included.

Getting better at anything involves stretching beyond our capabilities, but also letting our mind recover and adapt to the newly gained territory. Here we can use the analogy of building muscle. Weightlifting doesn't make the muscles grow; it only stimulates them to grow. The actual growth happens while we rest and recover, mostly during sleep. Similarly, practice stimulates our abilities to grow, but the adaptation, consolidation, and actual *growth* happens while we rest and recover. That means breaks, recovery, and sleep should be considered active components of getting better at anything and must be an integral part of our practice plan.

Build the Practice Habit

When we are starting out, we can rely on motivation and willpower alone to practice, but they can only take us so far. We need to build a solid habit to keep us going through the months and years of training ahead of us.

At their most basic, habits are an association between a cue, a response to that cue, and a result or reward from that response. If we practice first thing in the morning every day, we'll create an association between waking up and going to practice. Waking up is the cue, practice is the response, and the feeling of completion at the end is the reward.

Repeating the same cycle of *Cue > Response > Outcome** over time strengthens the action and makes it more unconscious. If we keep practicing every morning after waking up, the routine will turn into an automatic loop that takes care

---

* Cue > Routine > Reward was popularized by Charles Duhigg in his book *The Power of Habit: Why We Do what We Do in Life and Business*. It's also referred to as Cue > Craving > Response > Reward (with the extra step "Craving") by James Clear in his book *Atomic Habits: An Easy & Proven Way to Build Good Habits & Break Bad Ones*. I recommend both books for anyone interested in the subject.

of itself, and the more we repeat it, the less we resist it. We'll wake up in the morning and, without thinking about it or having to fight our excuses, head out to practice. That's the automation we are after.

The challenge with habits is that we can't reason our way into them. Knowing which habits we want in our lives (and even why we want them) is not enough. Only repeated action, going through the cycle over and over, can build our habit and eventually take it to a tipping point where it becomes easier to do it than not to. Let's look at some ways to help us do it.

Implementation plan. We are more likely to do something if we plan for when, where, and for how long we'll do it. If we want to write every day, our plan could be, "I'll sit at my desk to write every day from 8:00 a.m. to 10:00 a.m." In this example, we state specifically when, where, and for how long we'll write. At the same time, we are planning for consistency by doing our writing at the same time and location, making it more likely that it'll turn into a habit.

A variation for this implementation plan would be to use habits and routines we already have as "time" cues instead of specific hours in the day, such as "I will write after breakfast for two hours" (instead of "I will write from 8:00 to 10:00 a.m."). In this variation, we are turning the end of an established routine in our lives, having breakfast, into the trigger for our new habit, writing. Our implementation plan for writing would then look like this, "Every day after breakfast, I'll sit down at my desk and write for two hours."

This habit "stacking" (adding writing after breakfast in our example) is one of the most effective ways to build new habits. It takes advantage of the association principle by connecting what we want to do with something we are already doing.

With enough repetition, the "stacked" habits will form a chain where the first one automatically pushes us into the next one.

Rules. If we want to have an even more detailed implementation plan, we can add rules to it. These will be the things to do and *not* to do around our practice habits. Let's look at an example for someone learning golf.

> Rule 1: Practice Thursday through Sunday for a minimum of two hours per session.
> Rule 2: Don't go more than seven days without a coaching session.
> Rule 3: Study the games of the masters for two hours on Mondays.
> Rule 4: Document every game I play so I can study them.
> Rule 5: Study my own games within two days of having played them.

Rules can also follow "what if" scenarios—also known as "if/when–then" plans. In our example, they could be something like, "If I don't have a busy week, I'll practice an extra day on Wednesday." Or "If I feel stuck with a lesson, I will schedule another coaching session that same week instead of waiting for the next one." By defining the behavior and contingencies around our practice beforehand, we'll know what we are supposed to do at any given time, making it easier to follow through.

Our implementation plan can have as many rules as we want, but we need to be careful not to make it overwhelming. We should also add rules progressively. If we give ourselves many rules from the start, our practice can feel rigid. It's better to start with a few rules and add more as we get used to them.

First consistency then intensity. Habits get built through long-term consistency instead of short-term intensity. Many of us try to practice too much too often in the beginning, making it more likely that we burn out and quit. The right approach to building our practice habit is to focus on consistency first and adding intensity second—to start small and build upon it. An example would be to start with short practice sessions a few times a week for a month and then lengthen the sessions or add more of them per week once we've established the habit. This progression is more effective in building a new habit than trying to cram our way into it.

Rewards and penalties. Ideally, practice should motivate us. There should be no need for rewards or penalties. But the reality is that we'll go through times of frustration and discouragement, and we'll need an extra push. It's during these times that rewards and penalties can keep us going until we regain our intrinsic motivation.

On the rewards side, we should use something that encourages more practice. If you have the goal of painting every day, your reward could be to buy a new set of brushes or better-quality paint if you stick to your habit for a month. Using those new painting tools as a reward will encourage more painting and keep the habit going.

Opposite to rewards, some people find it easier to stick to a habit when facing a penalty for not doing so. This could mean donating to a cause you disapprove of, not eating your favorite snack for a week, or any penalty that comes to mind. It doesn't have to be harsh—even small penalties can go a long way.

Try rewards, penalties, or both if you are having trouble sticking to your practice habits and need the extra push, but make sure not to rely on them often. Going deeper into our craft and getting better at it should be our motivation to keep practicing—if it's not, we might be in the wrong field.

Rewards or penalties should only be used to give us a boost when we need it.

Get back on track as soon as possible. There will come a time when we'll break our practice habit. It happens. We'll miss a day or cut our practice short. That's normal, and we shouldn't beat ourselves up for it. Missing a day is not a big deal, but we should be careful not to let it snowball. What happens often is that we miss a few days and fall into what's been called "what the hell" mode. We think that since we already missed a day or two, all is lost, and there's no point in practicing for the rest of the week. We think, "I missed two days already. What the hell, I will start again next week." We should avoid this pattern at all cost; it will turn a small sidetrack into a derailment.

If we break our practice habits, we must get back on track as soon as possible—and not let it escalate into more missed practice. A great piece of advice from James Clear, author of *Atomic Habits: An Easy & Proven Way to Build Good Habits & Break Bad Ones*, is to be forgiving if we break our habit one day (in our case, missing a practice session) but never allow ourselves to break it twice in a row. Following this rule will keep us from going from missing a day of practice to missing a week or even a month.

Make your habit easy to stick to and hard to break. We have better chances of sticking to a habit if we make it convenient to do so and inconvenient to break. For those in bodybuilding, for example, a way to make their nutrition habits convenient is to prepare and freeze their meals in advance. When it's time to eat, they don't have to think about it; they take out their prepared meal and eat it. On the other side, a way for them to make it inconvenient to break proper eating habits would be not keeping "forbidden" foods in the house. It's hard to stick to a diet if you have a pot of *"dulce de leche* and brownie chunks" ice cream staring at you through the freezer drawer. But if you have to leave the house and go to a store to buy the ice cream, it's more likely you won't cheat on your diet.

We can use the same principle for a practice habit. If you are into sports, a way to make morning practice convenient would be to prepare your training clothes the night before. Having your gear ready to go takes away resistance from your habit. It's one less task to do before heading to practice, which translates into one less chance to ask yourself the downward spiral question, "Do I feel like doing it today?" The moment you ask that question, you already lost half the battle. The goal, then, is to reduce the chances of asking it by removing decisions and inconveniences around your desired habit.

As for making our practice habit difficult to break, we can copy the amazing writer Neil Gaiman. He reserves time for writing and sticks to a rule he set for himself: "You can sit here and write, or you can sit here and do nothing, but you can't sit here and do anything else." After a while of doing nothing, he explains, writing is more interesting, so he writes.

Depending on our craft and our circumstances, we'll have specific obstacles, decisions, and excuses that make it harder to stick to our practice habits. But the goal remains the same: to remove as many of them as we can. The more convenient and less mentally taxing we make things around our practice habit, the more likely we'll stick to it. And at the same time, the more inconvenient it is to break our habit, the less likely we are to do it.

———

Practice is how we turn knowledge into abilities. It's also the step where we'll spend most of our time. Learning and mastering a skill takes many hours of practice; that's the process. We can't escape that reality or take shortcuts, but we can use the principles and strategies we explored in this chapter to optimize our practice and get the most out of it.

Moving forward, we want to use our skills. We want to perform, compete, or simply enjoy doing what we've learned. But going from isolated practice and drills to performance is a big jump. We need to bridge the two steps and progressively transfer the abilities we developed during practice to their execution in performance. How do we build that bridge? Let's find out.

CHAPTER 8

Bridge

Plan for what is difficult while it is easy, do what is great while it is small.

—SUN TZU

Bridging (aka integrating practice) is the progression from practice to performance, a way to prepare for the "real thing" by practicing in realistic-yet-controlled settings. In that sense, bridging is an extension of practice but with the goal of transferring our abilities to real-world scenarios.

Bridging practice and performance is crucial for professions where stakes are high. Pilots, armed forces, emergency responders, and astronauts, to name a few, rely on bridging (simulations and rehearsals) to prepare for difficult situations. Since they don't have the luxury to make mistakes in real life, they need to put long hours into simulated missions and training to prepare for the real thing before it happens.

Retired Navy SEAL Leif Babin stresses the importance of bridging in his book *Extreme Ownership: How U.S. Navy SEALs Lead and Win*: "I don't think people realize the amount of rehearsals and walkthroughs we conduct before every operation." Navy SEALs don't just practice techniques and hope for the best once it's time to execute. They simulate missions and scenarios to be better prepared for when they face them in real life. Aside from improving their chances of success, it can also save their lives.

Bridging leads to better learning and, ultimately, better execution. High-stakes professions rely on it for a reason: it works. And while our craft may not involve the risks of military missions or piloting an aircraft, we'll benefit from bridging too. So, what are the principles of bridging? And what strategies can we use to take advantage of them? That will be the subject of this chapter.

THE PRINCIPLES

Transfer

Transfer in learning is the ability to take the skills we develop in one context and apply them in another. Let's look at boxing as an example. Boxers use training pads, shadowboxing, and heavy bags to work on their technique. They practice moves repeatedly, stopping and starting as needed, and removing variables so they can focus on a few things at a time. But a match is a different context than practice. Their opponent will move around and punch back, there are no do-overs, and a mistake can cost them the fight. It's not enough for boxers to develop a good technique then, they also need to transfer it to the context of a fight.

The challenge is that going from isolated practice to the pressure and complexity of a real match is too big of a jump. Boxers need a way to progress to "the real thing" while remaining in a controlled environment. That's where bridging comes in. Boxers bridge the gap between practice and performance by simulating fighting scenarios with their coaches and sparring with fellow boxers. This makes practice feel real enough to prepare for fights but safe enough to work on their technique and make mistakes without major consequences, the ideal progression for a successful transfer.

Simulation

We can divide bridging into two steps that move gradually toward performance: simulation and rehearsal. First comes simulation, which is practicing in realistic scenarios. In our boxing example, simulation could mean training punching combos with a coach as he moves around and pretends to punch back. This simulation would give us a better feel for how to use combos in a match while still in control of starting and stopping as necessary, repeating the moves as much as we want, and adjusting the speed of the drills just as we would during isolated practice with a heavy bag.

If we are learning a song on guitar, simulation could be practicing the song alongside the original track. This would force us to keep up with the tempo and adjust the details, so we play it as close to the real song as possible. In sports such as basketball or football, it could be done through plays and drills that resemble real games. Anything we do to make our practice more realistic is a form of simulation.

There are several benefits in using simulations. When we practice in a simulated environment, we get to see the use and value of what we are learning. Theory becomes relevant and concrete, making it easier to internalize. Simulation also provides a realistic but safe environment that offers us the freedom to try new things without fear of the outcome.

Another benefit of simulation is that we can use it to train for rarely occurring but important events. This is especially important for high-stake fields such as aviation. Fortunately, flight emergencies don't happen often, but that also means pilots have few opportunities to practice for them organically. They still need to learn how to deal with problems in case they happen, so they turn to simulations to do so. With flight simulators, pilots can practice emergency maneuvers and procedures over and over to develop their response skills—and keep them sharp—without endangering lives.

Simulation also works as a form of testing. By practicing in realistic scenarios, we can find out what we are doing right and what needs more work. When pilots go into simulated scenarios, they quickly realize if they are on top of their skill or not and then use that information to improve their training.

Though I'm using flight simulators as an example, simulation in our craft doesn't have to be sophisticated; it's only a matter of putting our practice in context and bridging it closer to how we'll execute it in performance. Let's turn now to rehearsals.

Rehearsal

The line between rehearsal and simulation is thin. Both forms of bridging center on recreating realistic conditions, but in simulation we are practicing individual parts of our skill (we choose specific things to work on, go over them repeatedly, start and stop as needed, and regulate the difficulty as we like), and in rehearsal we are putting everything together the way we would in a real performance.

In rehearsals, we are not stopping and starting often (or at all) and don't get to choose specific parts to work on. Instead, we bring ourselves as close to "real" conditions as possible while keeping the stakes low. Think of rehearsals as mock or trial performances. An example in racing sports would be to practice on the competition track as if it were the actual race. In public speaking and performance arts, it would be to perform in front of friends or test audiences. And in gymnastics, it would be executing a routine as if in real competition (referred in the sport as "pressure sets").

Let's take a closer look at the difference between simulation and rehearsal. In acting, *simulation* could be practicing lines with colleagues and recreating scenes. In this form of practice, the actor would go over parts of a play as much as needed, jump around, and tweak things. But in a *rehearsal*, the actor goes through the play the way it's meant to be performed.

In team sports, *simulation* can take the form of practicing plays and drills in realistic game conditions—but not playing an actual game. A *rehearsal*, however, would be playing exhibition games, intra-squad games, or practice games (also known as a scrimmage in certain sports). In these scenarios, players are not practicing one drill over and over, or starting and stopping as they like; they are playing an actual game, though without high stakes on the line.

Rehearsal, like simulation, offers the benefit of practicing in realistic conditions without hard consequences from our mistakes. It also tests our abilities and provides feedback on what we are doing right and what we need to improve. But rehearsal has an extra benefit compared to simulation: it moves us closer to performance and, in doing so, makes us better prepared for it.

THE STRATEGIES

Make It Look and Feel Real

Boxers train and spar in a ring, the environment where they will compete. Actors rehearse their plays on the stage where they will perform. Military personnel train with the equipment they will carry on the field. Astronauts train with their suits in diving tanks that simulate the low-gravity environments they will face. Bridging, whether simulation or rehearsal, is about making the conditions around practice look and feel closer to performance.

One way to create realistic scenarios is to role-play. This is especially useful for communication skills such as negotiation or sales, but it's also used in military training, medicine, and other domains. The idea is simple: we pick a scenario and play a role in it to practice for specific situations. In negotiation training, for instance, students divide into groups to represent the different parties of a simulated negotiation. And in sales, one person can play the role of a difficult or indecisive customer to force another to practice handling objections.

The same concept applies to other skills. In mixed martial arts, a sparring partner can play the role of different types of fighters (strikers, grapplers, southpaws). In chess, a partner can play the role of a defensive or aggressive player. And in competitive video games, practice partners can play different characters and adopt different playing styles to help us become more adaptable.

Another way to create realistic scenarios is to use test audiences—mentioned earlier. Comedians use these often. They go unannounced to venues to test new sets. It helps them prepare for performing in front of larger audiences. It also gives them feedback on how to adjust their delivery, order, or material. The goal with test audiences is not to perform; it's to fine-tune our skills and bridge the gap going into official performances.

Tweak the Rules

Tweaking the rules means distorting normal conditions of our craft to force ourselves to work on specific techniques or to manipulate the difficulty of our training.

Let's look at an example. Imagine we are learning basketball and want to improve on our three-point shots. We could practice shooting repeatedly from behind the three-point line. We could even interleave our practice by shooting behind the line from different distances and angles. But getting better at three-point shots in isolation is not enough. We also need to get better at everything that surrounds a three-point shot in a real game, such as finding space, moving into position, and shooting under pressure. That's where bridging comes in. We could simulate real game conditions in our practice (simulations) or play practice games (rehearsal).

Simulations in this scenario would be straightforward: three-point practice drills with marks, pressure, or moving into position from different parts of the court before shooting. But rehearsal (practice games) poses a problem. In a basketball game, we'll go for two-points more often than three, making it a suboptimal way for practicing our three-point shooting skills. So, how can we encourage the use of three-point shots in a real game environment and make it a valuable form of practice? We tweak the rules of the game.

One option would be to play practice or intra-squad games where the only shots allowed are threes. Or make three-pointers worth nine points and two-pointers worth one.

These tweaks will force us to practice our three-point shots while keeping us in a dynamic environment that resembles a real game.

We can apply the same strategy to anything else by following the principle behind it: creating circumstances that force us to work on specific parts of our skill. A great unintentional example of this strategy comes from Brazilian soccer players. When researchers set out to find what made Brazil a hotbed for soccer, they found a link between many of the country's great players and the time they played a small-scale version of the game while growing up, *futsal*. This version has similar rules to soccer, but it is played on a smaller field, forcing players to develop better control of the ball and precision in their passes and shots. And though *futsal* is a sport on its own, soccer players can use this version of the game to encourage practicing control and accuracy while staying in a realistic game environment.

Tweaking the rules is not reserved for sports. Drawing students work on their perception skills by copying images upside down. That's not the usual way to draw, but the practice is an effective way to learn one of the most important skills in drawing: seeing lines as lines (ignoring what the lines represent, and see them for what they are).

Tweaking the rules can also be used to manipulate the difficulty or complexity of what we practice. In the previous chapter we looked at the example of Josh Waitzkin; he learned chess starting from reduced complexity and endgame positions—scenarios with few pieces on the board resembling the game's end stages. This is not how a normal match goes; typically, players start with all pieces on the board in their setup positions. Waitzkin tweaked the rules and started with a few pieces in arbitrary positions so he could focus on specific parts of his game. We can copy his approach and apply it to our craft by following the principle behind it: remove variables or reduce complexity while remaining in real "play" conditions.

On the opposite side, we can also tweak rules to make practice harder than performance. Michael Phelps would sometimes swim in his sneakers, wearing a scuba vest, or tethered to a pulley. Wayne Gretzky would do drills with tennis balls because they are harder to control than hockey pucks. Lacrosse players train with sticks that have a smaller pocket (referred to as "fiddle sticks") so it's harder to catch the ball. And musicians apply the same concept by practicing pieces at a higher tempo than needed for performance.

The same can be done in our own craft. The principle to follow is to train in scenarios that are harder than what we'll face in actual competition or execution.

In this chapter, we've explored how to bridge the gap between practice and performance. We learned to use simulation and rehearsal to optimize the transfer of our abilities and progressively train for the "real thing." Here, we conclude the "learning *how* to do it" phase of the process. Now it's time to execute what we've practiced. It's time to perform.

CHAPTER 9

Perform

> I have been impressed with the urgency of doing. Knowing is not enough; we must apply. Being willing is not enough; we must do.
>
> —LEONARDO DA VINCI

Our vision of performing is what got us interested in a skill in the first place, and it's the reason for all our preparation. We've done our studying, our memorizing, our practicing, and our bridging; now, we finally put our abilities to use.

For our discussion, "performing" is executing our skills, either for our own joy, in competition, in front of an audience, in solitude, or in any other form. It's using what we know regardless of the setting.

Performance is not direct learning, but it supports it by reinforcing our knowledge, building our experience, and providing valuable insight into what needs additional practice. While this step in the process can seem straightforward, there are important points to explore. What's the difference between practice and performance? How is performance affected by our mindset? And what can we do to give a performance that reflects the best of our abilities instead of freezing when it matters most? That will be the subject of this chapter.

THE PRINCIPLES

Performance vs. Practice

We'll start our discussion by making an important distinction: performance is not practice. Our goal during practice (including bridging) is to develop our skills, and our goal during performance is to execute them. When we perform, we are not actively trying to learn; instead, we are letting our training take over and using what we already practiced as best as we can.

As an example, when musicians perform, they play what they already know. They are not using the time to learn the songs or work on their skills. Same goes for martial artists. During competition (performance), they are not trying to improve their technique—that came during practice and bridging. Their focus is on things such as strategy and timing: when to use the techniques, instead of how to do them. In the same line, during a football game, a quarterback is concerned with plays, open spaces, and avoiding interceptions rather than how to rotate his hips to generate more power—that groundwork should have come long before the game.

While performance gives us experience and reinforces our learning through repetition (when we perform, we are repeating what we know), it's not an alternative to practice. Practice requires the conditions we discussed in chapter 7, which are not present during performance. Remember: the purpose of performance is to use our skills, not to build them.

Great Performances Stand on Great Practice

There are countless hours of practice behind the great performances of the people we admire. We don't see it, but they spend more time and energy refining their skills than executing them. In the words of Usain Bolt, "Competition is the easy part, behind the scenes is where the work is done." Most of us want to do the opposite; we want to perform because it's more fun, more glamorous, or more interesting than training. It's also what got us into our craft in the first place. We visualized ourselves executing, not practicing. Those going into music, for example, imagine themselves playing their favorite songs, not sitting alone in a room working on chords and scales for hours. But that's what it takes to get good at playing an instrument.

"We don't rise to the level of our expectations," Archilochus noted. "We fall to the level of our training." We can't expect our skill to improve magically while we perform. The quality of our performance depends on the quality of our practice. So, if we want results when they matter most, we must invest time and effort into our preparation. As Michael Jordan once said, "I've always believed that if you put in the work, the results will come. I don't do things half-heartedly. Because I know if I do, then I can expect halfhearted results. That's why I approached practices the same way I approached games. You can't turn it on and off like a faucet. I couldn't dog it during practice, and then, when I needed that extra push late in the game, expect it to be there."

Performance and Mindset

Aside from technical preparation, the other key factor influencing our performance is our mental training. Without a strong mindset, even the most skilled among us can crumble under pressure and perform below our capabilities. Doubt, fear, anxiety, blocks, negativity, and criticism can get the better of us if we don't know how to deal with them.

Here, we are venturing into the world of sports psychology, a field that applies to optimal performance in any craft. The goal of this area of psychology is to help us develop the mental toughness and confidence to give our best, withstand pressure, and recover from difficult times. We sometimes refer to this as "inner game" training, and it includes meditation, positive beliefs, visualization, breathing exercises, self-talk, rituals, and motivation, among other things.

Peak performance and the mental training required for it, a skill on its own, are complex subjects beyond our discussion. We'll touch on them in this chapter and in those to come, but we won't go in depth. For those interested in learning more, I recommend looking into the work of Dr. Michael Gervais, the renowned sports psychologist behind the mental training of the Seattle Seahawks. Dr. Gervais is also famous for helping Felix Baumgartner to overcome anxiety and claustrophobia so he could set the world record for skydiving by jumping to earth from the stratosphere.

THE STRATEGIES

Trust Your Training

Many athletes describe feeling like spectators of their own performances, as if they had gone into autopilot. That's the state we are after. Contrary to practice, where it's important to remain conscious, in performances we want our unconscious to do most of the work. If we give attention to every detail, we'll interrupt the automation we've spent so long developing.

When we perform, we shouldn't micromanage, criticize, or be overly conscious of what we are doing. We've already put in the work to prepare; now it's time to trust our training and let it take over. As Jazz great Charlie Parker said, "You've got to learn your instrument. Then, you practice, practice, practice. And then, when you finally get up there on the bandstand, forget all that and just wail." Our aim during a performance is to let our abilities flow through us—to get out of our way so our mind and body can do what we've trained them to do.

Trusting our training also means sticking to it in the face of challenges. Armed forces go through extensive preparation and are taught to trust that training, even in frustration or despair, because it'll give them the best chances to succeed, and depending on the situation, survive.

Trusting our training is not always easy. When things get tough, we'll be tempted to drop what we've practiced and try something new, often making things worse. We see it in fighting sports where, after taking a blow or losing a round, fighters switch up their approach, hoping to turn the tables. They usually end up making more mistakes and giving an advantage to their opponent.

It takes discipline to follow our training, especially when the stakes are high and things are not going our way. But if we don't trust our training when it matters most, why put energy to go through it in the first place? Our training can't guarantee the results we want, but staying with it gives us the best chances of getting them.

Focus on What You Want, Not What You Don't Want

This strategy is straightforward, though sometimes hard to follow. We are not good at thinking in the negative. When we focus on what we don't want, we create mental images of that precise situation and steer our mind toward it. Take motorsports, for example. One of the key lessons for racing a car or a motorcycle is always to look where we want to go. If we fixate our view where we *don't* want to go, that's exactly where we'll end up.*

The same applies to performance in other fields: we go where our attention goes. If you are performing music and keep thinking, "Don't play the wrong note, don't play the wrong note," guess what will happen: you'll play the wrong note. For that reason, we must focus on the moves we want to make and the things we want to achieve, not on what we want to avoid. The difference is subtle, but it has been proven time and again to influence how well we perform.

Stay Present

A big source of distraction (and mistakes) when performing is thinking ahead or thinking back. When we wander away from the present moment, we can become haunted by the mistakes we've made or overwhelmed by the magnitude of what lies ahead. Both scenarios take valuable energy away from the task at hand. So, whenever we feel our focus shifting timeframes, we must bring it back to the present and do our best to keep it there.

One way to remain present is by changing our view of the performance from a single large block to a group of smaller,

---

* A phenomenon known as "target fixation."

more manageable pieces. Endurance athletes are a great example of this. If a marathon runner or triathlete thinks of the entire race, they can get discouraged and mentally exhausted. They have to concentrate on the current step, then the next one, and then the one after that.

Another good example is tennis. The game's structure and scoring system leads players to break down their performance into smaller pieces: one point at a time, then one game, then one set. We can apply the same concept to our own field. Concert pianists can think of their performance one music piece or subsection at a time; actors, one scene at a time; writers, one paragraph or chapter at a time; football players, one play at a time; and so on.

When the stakes are high and our inner doubt creeps in, breaking up our performance into smaller pieces is one of the best strategies we can use. The freediving world champion Mandy-Rae Cruickshank put it best when she said, "When I dive constant ballast, I don't think about breaking a record. I can't ever think about the whole dive. It's too overwhelming. I have to chunk it down, create tiny, clear goals, I go through kick cycles. The voice keeps count. I want to pay attention through one cycle, then the next, then the next. Keep the count, that's my only goal. If I keep the count, I can stay in flow for the whole dive." By staying present, we keep our mind free from judgment and expectation, and we get to put all our energy into what's important *now*.

Let Go of Mistakes

Related to the last strategy is moving beyond mistakes. As we just discussed, going into the past or the future while performing pulls energy away from the task at hand. But going into the past needs a closer look because it involves dwelling on mistakes we've made. This can create a self-feeding cycle of doubt and anxiety that will continue to affect our performance.

Here's the reality: we'll make mistakes during performances; it happens. Most of the time, they won't be a big deal. It's our reaction to them that creates a problem. We make mistakes, and instead of moving on, we fixate on them. We let them distract us from the present moment and become the filter through which we judge our entire performance. This fixation splits our attention between execution in the present and judgment of the past, making it more likely we'll mess up again.

Once we make a mistake, we can't go back to change it, and worrying about it won't make things any better. What we can do is prevent mistakes from escalating by letting them go and drawing our attention back to what's important now. Our attitude after making a mistake should be: learn what you must, fix what you can, and move on as fast as possible.

In theory, letting go of mistakes sounds simple, but we know in practice it's a different story. Let's borrow, then, from cognitive-behavioral psychology to help us get better at it. The field tells us that the power mistakes hold in our mind comes from thinking of them as defining, catastrophic, and beyond our capacity to deal with. The strategy to manage these thoughts is to counter them by reminding ourselves that our mistakes do not define us, that they are likely not as bad as we think, and that we can recover from them. In other words, that things will turn out fine most of the time—especially if we've prepared diligently. This attitude will encourage us to give our best and recover fast when we stumble. We'll be covering more on mistakes and our attitude toward them later in the book (chapter 11).

We started our process with learning *what to do*, which took us through understanding and memorizing. Then we moved into learning *how to do it*, which involved practicing and bridging. And now, we close with *doing it*, the performance, executing our skills and putting them to use.

In this chapter, we made the distinction between practicing and performing and looked at strategies to perform to the best of our ability, and it's here that we conclude the "Learn" section of the book.

It's time to shift our focus from learning to *improving*. For this, we'll gather and use feedback to fine-tune our abilities and training. We'll also explore how to overcome common obstacles so they don't hold us back in our pursuit of mastery. Let's improve.

PART II

IMPROVE

CHAPTER 10

Gather and Use Feedback

He who knows others is learned; he who knows himself is wise.

—LAO TZU

Feedback is the ultimate improvement tool. It's through feedback that we find out what we are doing right, what are we are doing wrong, and what needs fine-tuning. We need to gather feedback at every step of the learning process, from study through practice through performance. Then, we use it to refine both what we do and how we do it in each of them. That's how we improve our skills and our training methods. But what makes good feedback? How do we gather it? And how can we use it to get better at our craft? That will be the subject of this chapter.

THE PRINCIPLES

Process vs. Outcome Feedback

There are two types of feedback: one has to do with how well we do something (process feedback) and the other with the results we get from what we do (outcome feedback). Both are useful, but they require a different analysis.

Let's take hockey as an example. Many factors influence the results of a game, and the win doesn't always go to the better team. Players shouldn't rely only on the scoreboard to judge how well they played or to decide what needs to improve. A team could win a game despite a poor performance or lose it even though they played great. Outcomes matter, but they don't tell the full story. The team must also look at the process, how well they played, and if they are improving overall—despite the score.

The way this translates to other skills, such as art, is the difference between the quality of our work (process) and how well it's received (outcome). What some artists consider their best work is not always the most popular, but some of their lesser work becomes the public's favorite. This means an artist could be improving her skills, but not necessarily getting more praise. Basing her progress only on the popularity of her work would be a mistake. She needs to look at both the process and the results, as each provides valuable information.

Feedback Needs to Be Timely

The most important condition for good feedback is that we need to get it fast. The longer it takes to get feedback, the less effective it becomes. Imagine you are learning to sing but can't hear what you are singing until minutes later. Or imagine you want to paint, but you can't see the lines on the canvas until hours or days after you paint them. Such a delay would make it extremely difficult to get better at those skills.

While those examples are extreme, they are not far from the conditions we create for ourselves. Think of actors, dancers, or athletes who don't watch recordings of their performances until days or weeks later—or don't watch them at all. How can they expect to get better if they postpone or, worse, refuse to examine what they are doing and how they are doing it? Seeking feedback and insisting on getting it soon is how great performers speed up their progress. They want to know what they need to improve, and they want to know it fast.

Later in the chapter, we'll look into the strategies to help us shorten the "feedback loop," the time between taking action and assessing the results it creates. For the moment, the point to keep in mind is that feedback needs to be timely. When we shorten the feedback loop, we also shorten the time it takes to get better.

Feedback Needs to Be Taken Seriously, but Not Personally

It's easy to get fixated on "negative" feedback—the mistakes we make, the times we fail—and take them as a reflection of who we are. This obsession can start a cycle of self-defeat, doubt, and negativity. We must avoid those mental states by learning to separate the performance from the performer and be critical about the former but sympathetic for the latter. As big wave surfing legend Laird Hamilton advises, "Make sure your worst enemy doesn't live between your own two ears."

Feedback, especially "negative" feedback, is meant to be taken seriously but not personally. It is only a snapshot of our current ability. It shows us what we are doing right and what we are doing wrong at a moment in time, but it's not an assessment of who we are or a prediction of how far we can or cannot go. In that sense, we should use feedback to make improvements, not to judge our worth. Beating ourselves up about it doesn't make us any better; taking corrective action does. (We'll be discussing more on dealing with mistakes and failures in chapter 11.)

Feedback Needs to Be Concrete

For feedback to be useful, we need to translate it into concrete action. Great teachers and coaches follow this principle. They move away from giving general feedback such as "You're doing it wrong" to actionable advice like "Bend your knees more," "Rotate your body," or "Hold the paintbrush lower." This should be our guideline for all feedback: to move past a simple judgment of right or wrong, working or not working, and find the specific adjustments we need to make.

Feedback Needs to Be Followed by Action

Feedback could be timely, objective, and even concrete, but it's still useless if we don't act on it. This point can't be stressed enough: we need to take action on the feedback we get, and we need to do it soon after getting it. Two good examples from the world of sports come from Michael Jordan and Tiger Woods. Jordan used to stay after games to practice on things he felt didn't go well. And we've seen Woods replay a move after making a bad swing. They both wanted to correct their mistakes, and they wanted to do it right away, while everything was still fresh.

THE STRATEGIES

Set Metrics

Peter Drucker, a management consultant and author, popularized one of the most famous lines in business: "What gets measured gets managed." This is as true for business as it is for anything else. Having a way to track our progress and monitor what we do is a valuable feedback tool. When we track our expenses, it's more likely we'll respect a budget, and tracking what we eat helps us stick to a diet.

Objective metrics show us what's working, what's not, and what needs fine-tuning. Bodybuilders, for instance, have different metrics for their body, such as fat percentage, muscle mass, and literal measurements of body parts. They also measure their training in weight load, reps, and sets. Tracking these metrics gives them insight into their progress, how fast they are making it, and if they need to adjust their training and nutrition.

So, how do we choose which metrics to track in our craft? First, our metrics should be about *improvement*. Let's look at runners. They track their progress based on their personal records, clocking better times, and polishing their technique instead of focusing on winning or losing a race. Results in a competition are not always a reliable measure of improvement, so runners must put emphasis on specific parts of their skill and select objective metrics for it instead.

Next, we must choose what we want to improve. A soccer team wanting to play better first needs to decide what "playing better" implies. Let's imagine for a moment that making more passes is what the team decides will raise their game. So, how can they know they are getting better at it? What metrics can they use to track their progress? It could be the number of passes per game, the number of passes per player, or the average time players keep the ball.

The same goes for our craft. We must first decide what specific parts we want to improve and then choose metrics that would track our progress. Keep in mind that our metrics may not be as exact or intuitive as those in the above examples, but tracking less-than-perfect metrics is better than tracking no metrics at all.

As a final note, when analyzing our progress, we must remember that we don't improve on a straight line. Our abilities fluctuate in a range. This means improvement is about doing better than before on average, bringing up our range, and not about progress from one day to the next. We'll go through ups and downs, good days and bad, but as long as our range is improving, we are on the right track.

Prioritize What to Work On

When gathering feedback, we'll find many things to correct—especially if we are starting out in a craft. Our first instinct will be to try to fix all of it at once, but we must choose a few pieces, the most important ones, and work on those first.

Imagine practicing volleyball and having a coach yelling twenty different things we are doing wrong and need to correct. We would get overwhelmed and end up making more mistakes. We can't fix everything at the same time, and we shouldn't try to do so. Instead, we need to focus on what's most important to adjust right away and then progressively fine-tune the rest.

Prioritizing what to work on is especially important during performances, when our attention should be on executing our skill and not actively improving it. If we try to fix too much while performing, we'll take focus away from the present moment and break our "flow." There will be time later to look back and analyze everything we need to work on, but during the performance, we should only adjust the essential. Good coaches follow this rule. They know that if they coach too much during a game, it will make their players self-conscious and take away the concentration they need for the task at hand.

Test

We've discussed testing (practice retrieval) throughout the book, and we'll briefly touch on it again here for its value in providing feedback. To refresh your memory, testing can come in the form of quizzes, self-testing, drills, or anything that forces us to retrieve our knowledge from memory. As mentioned before, testing has the benefit of reinforcing our learning, but more related to our current discussion, it also helps us gather feedback. Through testing, we find out what we know, what we don't, and what needs fine-tuning. It's how we get a real assessment of our abilities so we can continue to improve them.

The Humble Mirror

Using mirrors is a common practice in many skills. Boxing, weight training, magic, public speaking, and dancing are a few examples. The mirror shows us what's right and what needs adjusting. But most valuable, it gives us this feedback instantly, allowing us to act upon it as we go. Without a mirror, we could do hours of practice only to find out later that our technique was wrong.

Using a mirror doesn't apply to every skill, but for those

where it does, it serves as one of the best feedback tools available. It's unfortunate that working with a mirror is undervalued even in skills where it can have the most impact. We will not make that mistake; we'll give the humble mirror the importance it deserves and use it whenever possible to assess and refine our technique.

Recordings

A related strategy to using a mirror is to record ourselves. The mirror's advantage is that it offers immediate feedback; we can see what we are doing as we are doing it. Recordings, however, have a longer feedback loop. We see what we are doing and how we are doing it only when we go back to check the recording. But what we lose in immediacy, we gain in perspective. Recordings give us a third-person point of view, which is often more objective. What's more, we can review recordings as much as we want and refer back to them when we need to.

Recording training sessions and performances has become common practice in many arts and sports. One example comes from Michael Phelps. "I went to Bob [his coach] and asked him for video of all my swims from Athens." Phelps wrote, "I took those videos and watched them over and over. When I watched one of the events, I understood clearly that I had gone out too slowly and that the third turn had left me at an impossible disadvantage. It was abundantly clear what I needed to fix."

Indeed, we can learn a lot from recording and analyzing what we do. Elite athletes such as Phelps, Kobe Bryant, Serena Williams, Simone Biles, and Tom Brady, to name a few, credit a great part of their improvement to analyzing their own performances. But the use and benefits of recordings are not limited to sports; they also apply to music, dance, sales, public speaking, and many other fields.

In working with recordings, we must aim to follow the principles of good feedback: studying the recordings soon after we finish them (to keep the feedback loop short), not taking our mistakes personally, emphasizing concrete pieces we need to work on, and taking corrective action as soon as possible.

As an extra step, we can analyze our recordings in comparison with recordings of advanced practitioners. This is especially useful for sports and motor skills. The idea is to look at our practice or performance side-by-side, or in succession, with that of people better than us. This will help us identify what we need to do differently and what to adjust in our technique.

A word of caution: Watching recordings of our practice or performance will be uncomfortable at first. We'll tend to focus on everything we're doing wrong and may get discouraged by it. But we need to move past this feeling and remember that even though we don't like what we see, we are doing it to get better—and it will make us better. Going through discomfort so we can improve is preferable to repeating the same mistakes for years because we didn't have the courage to take an honest look at ourselves.

Fresh Perspective

"We clearly know that errors are recognizable more in the works of others than in our own," Leonardo da Vinci wrote, "and often, while finding fault with the minor errors of others, you will ignore your own great ones." To overcome this blind spot and have a more objective view of our work, Leonardo recommends that we look at it from a fresh perspective.

His approach was to put a mirror next to the painting he was working on to see it reversed. Leonardo also advises painters to step away temporarily from their work and "take a little recreation elsewhere," such as going for a walk, because once they come back to it, they will have better judgement. Additionally, he suggests that they place themselves at a distance from their painting so they can see it from a different perspective, figuratively and literally. In all cases, the goal is the same: to break the familiarity we have developed with our work so we can perceive it as if it were someone else's (or as if we were looking at it anew) and see the faults we might otherwise miss.

In many skills, we can access this fresh perspective by reviewing recordings of our practice and performance. We discussed this strategy above (recordings), but here we'll add an extra step. Aside from checking our recordings as soon as possible, we'll add additional review sessions spaced out over a few days.

In checking our recordings for the first time, what matters most is that we do it soon. We need to get feedback fast so we can start making corrections. The drawback here is that we are still too close timewise to the practice or performance we recorded, making it hard to take a detached look at it. To compensate for this downside and gain a fresh perspective, we'll review our recordings *again* days later. By then, we'll have less of an emotional attachment and can see our work (practice or performance) with clear eyes, noticing things we missed the first time.

With skills where we can't use recordings, we could do exactly as Leonardo suggests: we could look at our work from another angle or temporarily walk away from it to regain perspective. Artists could take the piece they are working on into a different room to see it under a new light. They could also cover it for a few days, so when revealed again, it looks "fresh."

The same goes for writers. They could read a piece they are working on in different environments or put it away for a few days before coming back to it. This latter approach is part of Stephen King's process. In his book *On Writing: A Memoir of the Craft,* King explains that once he finishes a novel, he puts it away for a while, so once he comes back to it, he can experience it from a fresh perspective. "You'll find reading your book over after a six-week layoff to be a strange, often exhilarating experience," King says. "It's yours, you'll recognize it as yours...and yet it will also be like reading the work of someone else, a soul-twin, perhaps. This is the way it should be, the reason you waited. It's always easier to kill someone else's darlings that it is to kill your own." When we take distance from our work, we can come back to it and see it in a new light. This fresh perspective becomes a wealth of insight to improve it.

Another way to gain a fresh perspective is through other people. Artists in many fields throughout history have relied on close friends, partners, or mentors to review their work and give them feedback. We all need quality opinions, and they shouldn't come solely from our own judgment, regardless of how good we are. A fresh pair of eyes will help us see mistakes we've turned blind to. It's the reason writers work with editors and musicians with producers. There's only so much we can see, so if we want to go beyond our limited view, we'll need to borrow the eyes of others.

Guidance

Mentors—coaches, teachers, instructors—play a major role in how we use feedback to improve. While mirrors, recordings, or fresh perspectives are great ways to collect feedback, the information we gather is only useful if we know how to interpret it. Here's where mentors become essential. They have the experience to notice what we can't, the knowledge to teach us what we need, and the wisdom to guide us through the process. Mentors help us push our abilities by not only pointing out what needs to be corrected but also giving us insight into how to do it. If we want to make the best out of the feedback we gather, we need a mentor on our side. (We'll be discussing more on mentors in chapter 13.)

Debrief, Analyze, and Document Your Work

Debriefing is about reflecting on our practice or performance after the fact. The idea is to analyze what happened, how it happened, and get as much feedback as we can. We can debrief by talking to our coaches or training partners, or even just reviewing everything in our mind. But if we want to get the most benefit out of debriefing, we must do it in writing—using a journal to document our work and our progress.

The more linear and organized nature of writing (as compared to talking) provides structure to our thoughts and helps us remember more details, promoting further insight in turn. It's not a coincidence that some of the greatest minds in history shared the discipline of documenting their work. Darwin, Newton, and Ben Franklin are some examples, and one that comes on the extreme is Thomas Edison, who wrote close to five million pages of notes relating to his sixty-year career as an inventor and businessman.

Aside from documenting the details of our practice or performance, we should also keep track of our results. Earlier, we talked about using metrics to measure our progress; here, we'll keep thorough notes on how we measure against them. This could mean keeping track of your time on a 400m butterfly if you are a swimmer, or your body composition and bicep size if you are a bodybuilder. Keeping good records of our progress not only serves as valuable feedback but also as proof of how far we've come, a valuable motivation aid during times of challenge and self-doubt.

Debriefing, documenting our work, and keeping track of our progress can be simple or complex, depending on our preference. Tiger Woods, for instance, is said to keep a record of every practice for future reference, noting down what worked, what didn't, and what to do differently next time. The more elaborate the analysis, the better. But if it feels overwhelming, start small and build upon it. For those ready to go in depth and get the most out of this strategy, here are some questions to use in your debrief:

- How did the practice/performance go overall?
- What went well?
- What went wrong?
- What do I want/need to improve first?
- Is there something I need to do more of?
- Is there something I need to do less of?
- Is there something I need to leave out?
- Is there something I need to add in?
- Is there something I need to balance?
- What is one thing I can do differently next time?
- Based on my metrics, am I on the right path?

This detailed debriefing leads to better feedback. Questions such as "What should I add in?" or "What should I leave out?" are useful because sometimes we find solutions to problems by adding or removing something instead of changing it entirely. But we can't find these fixes if we are vague in our analysis. Thinking, "Practice didn't go well. I need to improve," is not enough; we need to dig deeper. Why didn't it go well? What changes might improve it? Is it something I'm not doing? Is it something I'm doing too much or too little of? This detailed analysis results in more useful insight.

Retired Navy SEAL Leif Babin writes about the importance of doing such an analysis: "The best SEAL units, after each combat operation, conduct what we call 'post-operational debrief.' No matter how exhausted from an operation or how busy planning for the next mission, time is made for this debrief because lives and future mission success depend on it."

And it is not a shallow debrief, either, as Leif continues to explain, "A post-operational debrief examines all phases of an operation from planning through execution, in a concise format. It addresses the following for the combat mission just completed: What went right? What went wrong? How can we adapt our tactics to make us even more effective and increase our advantage over the enemy?"

This analysis requires discipline and dedication. The payoff, however, is well worth the effort. Leif then concludes, "Such self-examination allows SEAL units to reevaluate, enhance, and refine what worked and what didn't so that they can constantly improve."

Though most of us won't face the high-stakes situations of Navy SEALs, doing detailed debriefs and analysis will still provide immense value in our path. It is tedious work, yes. It also takes time and won't always be fun, but it leads to greater improvement.

In this chapter, we've learned how to gather feedback and use it to improve. This is not a step in the learning process, but something we must do at every stage. Whether we are studying, practicing, memorizing, or performing, we rely on feedback to know what's working and what needs to be fine-tuned or changed—both in what we do and how we do it. It is through this constant loop of taking action, analyzing the results, and making adjustments over time that we reach higher levels in our craft.

But gathering and using feedback is only one side of improvement. We'll face challenges in our journey that can halt our progress if we don't know how to deal with them. In our next chapter, we'll explore common obstacles in pursuing a craft and the strategies to overcome them.

CHAPTER 11

Overcome Challenges

> The ultimate measure of a man is not where he stands in moments of comfort and convenience, but where he stands at times of challenge and controversy.
>
> —MARTIN LUTHER KING JR.

Everyone who has pursued a craft had to deal with difficulties and discouragement along the way. They faced failures, mistakes, boredom, impatience, blocks, and plateaus. We'll face these challenges, too, and not only once, but time and again as we learn and refine our skills. It's part of the process.

"What people tend to forget is the journey that I had getting to Formula One," says multiple-time world champion Lewis Hamilton. "There were plenty of years where I had to learn about losing and having bad races." If we want to improve and stay on the path of mastery, we must learn how to respond to adversity. Our goal won't be to avoid such obstacles—that's impossible—but to prepare for when they come. So, what are the toughest challenges we'll face? And how can we overcome them? That will be the subject of this chapter.

THE PRINCIPLES

Setbacks

Mistakes and failures are a common reason to give up a craft. They are discouraging and can damage our self-image, but they are a natural part of learning and mastering any skill. Think of anything you learned in life; it's likely you didn't get it right the first time. You made mistakes and failed. It's part of the process. And as much as we don't like setbacks, they play an important role in learning. Mistakes and misses teach us what we need to improve, where to direct our focus, and even how to do better next time. In the words of Thomas Edison, "Negative results are just what I want. They're just as valuable to me as positive results. I can never find the thing that does the job best until I find the ones that don't."

The challenge with setbacks is how we respond to them. We tend to take them as a reflection of who we are and as a measure of our capabilities. We think, "I am a failure," or "I'll never be good at this," when the narrative should be "I failed. I'm not good at this *yet*, but I can learn from this experience and use it to be better next time." Imagine if we had the former toxic attitude while we were growing up; we wouldn't know how to walk, talk, ride a bicycle, read, or anything else. We would have given up after the first stumbles.

Part of the unhealthy relationship we have with mistakes and failure comes from unrealistic expectations. We think that if we are making mistakes and taking too long to improve, it's because we "don't have what it takes," and then use that as a reason to quit.

We also measure our progress in outcomes. In sports, for instance, we focus on winning or losing when we should be concerned with how well we performed. Remember: our goal must be improvement; winning will be a byproduct. Losing a game or a race is not a failure if we are doing better than before. "I don't mind losing as long as I see improvement or feel I've done as well as I possibly could," Olympic gold medalist Jackie Joyner-Kersee said. "If I lose, I just go back to the track and work some more."

Let's say you play tennis, and, in a recent match, you played the best tennis you've ever played. But let's also say your opponent was better and won. The way you process that event will impact your motivation and the way you see your abilities. On one side, you can focus on how well you played, the improvements you've made, and what you need to do to play even better next time. Or, on the other, you can focus on having lost the match, think of it as a failure, and beat yourself up about it. Nobody likes to lose or miss their mark, but we must be mindful of our attitude when it happens. It can be the defining factor to stay on track and master our craft, or a reason to quit it.

So, how can we develop a better relationship with our (inevitable) setbacks? First, we must see our mistakes and perceived failures as experience. Let's stay with our tennis example. In learning the sport, you will lose a lot of games...a lot. These are not useless "failures," however. These games are experience—especially if you gather feedback from them. Every game you play, whether you win or lose, adds to your knowledge of playing styles, tactics, and the game itself, making you better in the long term.

Second, we make mistakes and fail more often when we are at the edge of our skill. They are proof that we are testing our limits, and that's a good thing. If we are not making mistakes, it's likely we are in our comfort zone and not pushing ourselves hard enough. As Nobel laureate in physics Frank

Wilczek once put it, "If you don't make mistakes, you are not working on hard enough problems. And that's a big mistake."

This doesn't mean we should go out and make mistakes or fail for the sake of doing it. The point is that mistakes and failures are a side effect of pushing our limits, and our goal should be to get better at recovering from them instead of trying to avoid them. In the words of tennis great Serena Williams, "I really think a champion is defined not by their wins but by how they can recover when they fall."

Finally, we must also adopt the attitude Michael Jordan lives by, "I can accept failure, everyone fails at something, but I can't accept not trying." We need to embrace setbacks as a requirement of pursuing mastery and consider the only "failure" not to try, not to put in the work, or to walk away at the first sign of difficulty.

Impatience

Another challenge we'll face at different stages in our path is impatience. Starting out, our impatience will be about how long it takes to get better. This feeling often comes from unrealistic expectations. We forget that even masters had to start from nothing and follow the same path. Picasso had to learn to draw before becoming a great painter, and Bach had to learn chords before composing his masterpieces. Everyone begins as a beginner, and everyone has to go through intermediate stages before reaching an advanced level. It's a long process, and though some move through it faster than others, no one escapes it. We won't either.

It takes time to learn a craft, much more than we'd like to think. An example of this is learning to play musical instruments. It takes a while from the moment we start to when we can make half-decent sounds, let alone play through a song. This is not what we want to hear when we begin, but it's a reality we must accept. If we fight it and become impatient, we'll start jumping from method to method or teacher to teacher looking for an easier, faster way to get results. And though there's nothing wrong with searching for efficiency, if we don't commit to any practice for some time, our search for "a better method" creates a paradox: we spend so much energy switching our approach that we never work on getting better.

Impatience will also come at later stages in our path in the form of boredom. With time, the novelty of our craft will wear off, and we'll get tired of practicing the same thing over and over...and over again. Our boredom will tempt us to practice new, though many times useless, things to feel novelty again—like flashy techniques or moves we want to learn "just in case" or "just for fun." We must push through this boredom and stick to practicing what matters most, even when it feels "old." If we start chasing novelty, we'll never reach the higher levels of our craft.

Impatience can also take the form of frustration. We'll eventually hit plateaus, and sometimes they will last long enough to overrun our patience. But as frustrating as they are, plateaus are a normal part of learning any skill. We must learn to accept and work through them as they come. Let's take a closer look.

Plateaus

Plateaus are periods where there's little or no improvement (real or perceived) in our abilities. They can be discouraging because they feel like stagnation—no matter how much we practice we don't seem to get better. But there's more to plateaus than what we see on the surface. Let's discuss the different types and why they happen.

Consolidation plateaus. A consolidation plateau is a time where there's no perceived improvement. We are putting in the work and pushing ourselves to get better, but it feels as if we are not making any progress. Our feelings are not necessarily right, though. It takes time to internalize new abilities, and what sometimes looks like stagnation is a process of solidifying what we know. During consolidation plateaus, we are internalizing, strengthening, and automating parts of our skill so we can free conscious energy to build upon them. This phase is not as gratifying or evident as when we see expansion, but it's still progress—only that it happens "behind the scenes."

Comfort-zone plateaus (aka OK plateaus). These plateaus are when we are actually stagnant. These are not consolidation periods, but "we-are-no-longer-trying-hard-to-improve-anymore" ones. We fall into these plateaus for one of two reasons. One, we feel good about the level we've reached and want to stay in that comfort zone instead of challenging ourselves—we've become complacent. Or two, we've fallen into repetition mode. We show up to practice but just go through the motions as if on autopilot instead of engaging in deliberate practice—we've become detached.

Equipment plateaus. These plateaus happen when the equipment we are using puts a barrier to our progress. If our craft relies on a piece of equipment, there's only so much we can do without the proper one. If we are into photography, for instance, having to use a smartphone instead of high-quality cameras and lenses will limit our development and creative expression. The same principle applies to motorsports: if we never upgrade to a more powerful machine, we won't be able to push our limits and we'll eventually plateau.

This is not to say that tools make the master; that's never the case. Masters can do amazing things even with limited equipment. A great painter can make beautiful art with a single brush, a great photographer can take outstanding photographs with an average camera, and a professional motorcycle racer can make amateurs eat dust with a mediocre bike. But, for the focus of our discussion, having access to equipment that promotes our progress instead of hindering it will make a difference in how fast we improve.

Technique plateaus. These plateaus are caused by poor form, bad habits, or wrong technique. In playing string instruments, for instance, incorrect fingering can prevent us from playing fast pieces or getting the best sound out of our instrument. In weightlifting, the wrong technique will keep us from lifting heavier weights—and doing so without getting injured. And in golf, a flawed swing will hold us back regardless of how much time we spend hitting balls.

Depending on how much we need to correct, this plateau can be the most challenging to overcome. We'll need to unlearn and relearn parts of our technique so we can start making progress again. At the same time, since we are changing the way we've been doing things—the way we were already proficient at—we'll often get worse before we get better, a tough psychological position that will add to the already challenging situation.

A good example of this plateau comes from Tiger Woods. He changed his swing several times in his career because he felt the previous one was holding him back. Each time he changed his swing, his performance suffered before it got better. In his words, "I took some steps backward to go forward, to make some giant leaps forward." It takes courage and trust to take those steps back, and that's exactly what it took for Woods to overcome his limits—and later in his career, his injuries. It's also what it will take for us to overcome our own technique plateaus. We have to be willing to "let go of the good to get the great."

THE STRATEGIES

Manage Expectations

Unrealistic expectations are the cause of a lot of frustration in learning a craft. If we had a better idea of what to expect during the learning process, the time it takes to get better at our skill, and the common setbacks we'll face, we would be more forgiving of our mistakes and more patient throughout the process.

As a personal example, I went to a motorcycle racing training over a weekend. Moto racing is a challenging, thrilling, and sometimes dangerous sport. At the end of my first day, I took a turn too fast, lost control of the motorcycle, and fell hard. I hit the ground headfirst and rolled several times before I came to a stop. Everything happened in a flash, and I had no idea how badly I'd fallen. I was scared. I remained still for a while, worried I might have broken something and would make things worse by trying to stand up. Luck was on my side that day, and somehow, I walked away unharmed, physically at least—though I cannot say the same for the bike.

Almost immediately, I became afraid of riding a motorcycle again. I kept playing the fall over and over in my head, and every time, it made me more terrified of going back to the track. But I still had another day of training and wanted to finish what I had started—I also didn't want my motorcycle racing experience to end like that. So, against common sense, I went to the track again the next day.

When I saw my teacher, I told him about my fall from the day before, making a big deal out of it—which, in my mind, it was—but he didn't give me the sympathy I was expecting. "There are two types of riders," he said, "those who have fallen and those who are about to fall. It's great that you got your first fall out of the way. Now you know what it's like."

Riders fall off their bikes learning and practicing the sport—it happens. I didn't know this. I thought falls were rare and had made a drama out of mine, to the point where I considered quitting my training. It turned out I had not been the only "idiot," as I thought of myself, who fell on the track the first day. Eight other riders from different classes had fallen too. And it also turned out I was not the only "lucky bastard," as I also thought of myself, who had walked away unharmed. Most of them were fine. Had I known that falling wasn't a big deal and that sometimes it happens in the sport, I would have avoided the self-loathing, the fear, and the endless rants to my friends that night of how I had cheated "death."

Our expectations create a filter through which we see the world and ourselves, and the same is true in learning skills and judging our abilities. If we have the wrong idea of what it's like to learn our craft, we may get discouraged once we face reality. Our best strategy is to find out early what to expect in our journey (the exploration we did in chapter 4). We can do this by talking to people in our craft—teachers, practitioners, professionals—and asking them about the difficulties, time investment, and commitment needed to learn the skill. And though we shouldn't take their answers as absolute, they will give us a good idea of what we are getting into and help us prepare to deal with the challenges to come…for they will come.

Separate the Performance from the Performer

We are not our mistakes and failures. They don't define our capabilities. But most of the time, we find it hard to separate the performance from the performer—us. We take setbacks personally, dwell on them, and let them define us. We must remember, however, that analyzing our shortcomings should be a constructive task, not a destructive one. We are meant to find the lessons within our faults, and then move on. In the words of the writer Samuel Beckett, "Ever tried. Ever failed. No matter. Try again. Fail again. Fail better."

Making a mistake or failing doesn't mean we are not "talented," or that we'll never "get it," or even worse, that we should quit. It only means we are not "there" yet, that we need to get better. Once we learn to separate our outcomes from our identity, we'll gain the freedom to push ourselves and take risks without having our ego on the line. We'll also be more receptive to learning what we need to keep improving. This is the attitude of LeBron James, who said, "I try to put myself in a mental state of, 'How do I learn from that defeat? How do I learn from that loss?'" Our goal is to do better next time, and we can't do that if we spend our energy feeling bad for the past. Yes, not taking setbacks personally is easier said than done, but it's a worthwhile effort.

Keep in mind that not taking mistakes and failures personally doesn't mean not taking responsibility for them. Most of the time, we are solely responsible for our results. The point is that we don't have to get stuck in them. We also get to be responsible for how we react to those results. We can learn from them, correct what needs correcting, and keep moving forward. A good example of this attitude comes from chess grandmaster Garry Kasparov. "Mostly I lost games because I made terrible mistakes. I was very angry with myself, not with my opponents, with myself," he said. "It's my own fault. I always look at my losses, my defeats, as my personal fault. And all I had to do was just work more, just go back to the table, to the chess set and get better."

Remember Past Success

If we are haunted by mistakes or failures from the past and can't let go of them, one way to fight back is to remember past successes. "Negative" thoughts are constantly with us, like all the times we've messed up and everything we haven't achieved. What's less obvious is how far we've come, and all the things we've done right. We are terrible at keeping track of our successes or taking the time to remember them. But that's what we need to do to stay motivated and push through difficulties. How do we do this? A good option is to keep a journal of our achievements and review it often. When we have written evidence of our progress, we can come back to it at any time and balance the self-doubt that comes from ruminating on our setbacks.

Slow Down, Take a Step Back

We discussed earlier in the chapter that mistakes and failures will come when we push the boundaries of our level. In the words of Goethe, "Man will err as long as he strives." If we succeed all the time, we are not pushing ourselves hard enough. In sports, for instance, if we win all our games or competitions, we are likely not facing strong-enough opponents. But on the opposite side, if we are making many mistakes or failing often, we might be pushing ourselves too far or too fast.

Improvement happens when we practice at the edge of our

comfort zone, where things are challenging but within our reach. Let's use batting as an example. If we can hit every pitch at a certain speed range, we need to increase the difficulty—making practice challenging again. But if we are missing most of the pitches or breaking form, we need to slow down and lower the difficulty. What we are looking for is a place where things feel challenging but not impossible or overwhelming. If we are making many mistakes or we are sacrificing form, it's time we slow down and take a step back.

Trust the Process

Learning anything comes with its share of impatience, frustration, and sometimes boredom. It's unavoidable. But so is progress if we are diligent in our practice. If we put in the time and effort, we will get better. We must trust the process and not get discouraged when we don't see immediate results. As Jimi Hendrix once said, "Sometimes you are going to be so frustrated you'll hate the guitar, but all of this is just a part of learning. If you stick with it you're going to be rewarded." No skill, regardless of how difficult, can resist a relentless attack of deliberate practice. And even though the day-to-day actions may not seem to have an impact, when compounded over months and years, they build into mastery.

We must also remember that world-class artists, athletes, and communicators are not made overnight; they work at getting better every day over a long time. Writer William Zinsser put it best in his book *On Writing Well* when he wrote, "Nobody becomes Tom Wolfe overnight, not even Tom Wolfe." That is the perfect mantra to keep in mind when impatience is getting the best of us.

Trusting the process also means avoiding changing our

approach often. Impatience can make us jump from method to method looking for faster ways to get results. This endless search for greater efficiency can turn into a trap.

Let's look at fitness as an everyday example. Getting in shape takes time, discipline, and work. But nobody wants to hear that. People want—and look for—pain-free, fast, and easy methods. And they often change from one to another in search of the "perfect" one.

The reality is that many approaches work. And while some are more efficient than others, sticking to a decent diet and exercise routine is better than jumping from one to the next, not giving any of them enough time to work. The other reality is that even if there were a perfect method to get in shape, it would still involve diet or exercise in some form, and most likely both—that's the foundation of fitness. The process can be made more efficient, but it can't be escaped.

The same applies to our craft. Impatience can make us lose focus. It will tempt us to look for easier and faster methods and to change our practice and our teachers before giving them a chance. Or even worse, it can cause us to postpone getting started until we find that "perfect" approach—which will never come.

This doesn't mean we shouldn't look for efficiency. In fact, the premise of this book is to optimize learning. What we should be against is the trap of jumping from method to method in search of a magic pill. We must remember that just as diet and exercise are the foundation of getting in shape—and can't be avoided even with the most efficient approaches—practice (lots of it...for a long time) is the foundation of mastering a craft. That's the process, and no method can make us skip it. Pursuing false promises of shortcuts and jumping ahead will only take away precious time we could be using to improve.

Break Through Plateaus

"There are no limits," martial arts legend Bruce Lee said. "There are only plateaus, but you must not stay there, you must go beyond them." Earlier in the chapter, we explored the different types of plateaus and what causes them. Let's take a moment now to discuss how to deal with each.

In consolidation plateaus, we are putting in the effort and following the principles of deliberate practice, but it looks as if we were not making progress. This is because it takes time to solidify the newly gained level in our skills before we can level up again. Our improvement might not be noticeable—which can be discouraging—but it's happening. We are building more robust neural pathways to support improved performance. Consolidation plateaus, then, are dealt with patience and consistency. We must stay with our practice and trust the process. It's important, however, to get the help of a coach or mentor to make sure our technique is correct and that we are, in fact, in a consolidation plateau, not a technique one.

In comfort-zone plateaus, we are not making progress, but it's because we are not pushing ourselves hard enough. Maybe we started slacking in our practice, not being consistent, or falling into autopilot and simply going through the moves. We recognize we are in this plateau when practice doesn't feel challenging—and has become habitual instead. We also recognize it by taking an honest look at how much time we are dedicating to practice and how engaged we are in it. Deep down, we know if we've been giving our all or if we have just been showing up. We deal with comfort-zone plateaus by demanding more of ourselves and making practice challenging again.

Here, as in consolidation plateaus, coaches or mentors are of great help. They can see from the outside if we are reaching beyond our comfort zone, and if we aren't, they will push us to do so.

In equipment plateaus (specific to crafts where equipment plays a major role), it's our tools or gear that are limiting our progress. Most of the time, it will be intuitive that we've outgrown our equipment, but we can also find out with the help of a coach or mentor. Alternatively, we can try out better equipment and see if we are ready for it—or if it makes a major difference in our results. If, indeed, we are in an equipment plateau, we'll break through it by making the upgrade.

Finally, in technique plateaus, we are not making progress because of how we are doing things—problems with our technique. These plateaus are hard to identify as they can be mistaken with consolidation plateaus. The best way to know we are in a technique plateau and get past it is with the help of a coach or mentor. He or she can look at what we are doing and recognize if there are major issues with it. If we don't have access to a coach, we can check for problems using the feedback strategies from earlier in the book (i.e., recording ourselves or using a mirror). Once we find what's wrong, we'll need to refine it, correct it, or change it.

In this chapter, we've covered the common challenges we'll face along our path to improvement: setbacks, impatience, and plateaus. They will be a constant attack on our progress, but we now have strategies to move past them. Remember: It's not about trying to avoid challenges—they are unavoidable. It's about learning to overcome them.

Here, we conclude the "Improve" section of this book. We've learned how to improve our skills through feedback, and to confront the common challenges that can hold us back. But what if we want to go further? What if we want to chase the edge of our potential? What if we want to master our craft?

PART III

MASTER

CHAPTER 12

Elements of Mastery

> I hope you will disdain mediocrity and aim to excel in whatever you do.
>
> —VERA RUBIN

Mastery holds a special place in our mind. We look up to masters and admire their abilities as almost supernatural. In a technical sense, however, mastery is simply a (high) level in the learning spectrum—achieved through extensive study, practice, and refinement. We start as beginners, go through intermediate stages, pass by advanced ones, and then move into mastery.

But mastery means more to us than being exceptionally good at a skill. It has a magical quality to it. Masters fuse with their craft. Their skill flows with captivating grace. They notice details most of us miss, have a refined intuition that gives them an edge, and can adapt to changing circumstances while still delivering consistent results.

We recognize mastery when we see it; what's hard is putting all it means into a definition—much less one everyone would agree on. Mastery is too complex to be reduced, too great to be contained. So instead of trying to force it into a statement, let's explore the different elements recurrently present in mastery. That, I believe, is a better discussion that will also provide us with a clearer goal to aim at.

High-Level Proficiency and Consistency

The first element of mastery is *proficiency*—the ability to execute a skill and do it well. Masters are fluent in their craft. They have dedicated enough time to learn the conceptual and practical side of it. But beyond that, we regard masters as such for standing out from the majority through comparison or competition. They have high-level proficiency.

Related to proficiency is *consistency*. Masters are consistently good at what they do. They are not perfect. They still make mistakes, have bad days, and fail. But they perform at high levels most of the time. This is an important distinction. Masters don't become masters by doing something great once. It's not about a single game, a single art piece, or a single song. Instead, the mark of masters is in the long-standing, recurrent show of superior abilities.

In tennis, for instance, sometimes a top player will lose matches against lower-rank ones. This usually happens when the top player's bad day coincides with the lower-rank players' great ones. But in a longer timeframe, the top player will win more matches and more tournaments. For the top player, being on fire is the norm and playing badly the exception while for the rest, being on fire is the exception. When considered over a wide context, masters perform at top level an intimidating large amount of the time.

Sophisticated Memory and Mental Representations

In the memory chapter (chapter 6), we talked about chess masters and how they see the game in terms of patterns and higher structures that tell a story, while beginners see a scramble of pieces. Chess masters can see patterns and interpret their meaning due to the accumulated practice and study of the game. They also develop more sophisticated mental frameworks, allowing them to chunk information and memorize moves, positions, and arrangements with ease.

Some experts believe that chess masters' outstanding skills result from developing their memory for the game. Whether or not that's the case, what's clear is that all chess masters share a complex memory for playing chess built through a great amount of practice and experience. And we can say the same for masters in any craft. All masters have sophisticated mental representations for their skill, resulting in a superior memory for it. In Dr. Ericsson's words, "In pretty much every area, a hallmark of expert performance is the ability to see patterns in a collection of things that would seem random or confusing to people with less well developed mental representations."

Experience

No master is created in a vacuum. All of them had to go through a long journey to build their experience. Over time, this experience changes the way they process information. For chess players, every match becomes a valuable reference for future games. It's like building a chess pattern "database." And the more information they feed the "database," the better they can play.

Experienced players look at a chessboard through the filter

of all the games they've played before; they really see a different board than the rest of us. So, every time they recognize a pattern, their mind goes, "Been there, seen that," and chooses the best moves based on that experience. When David Epstein, author of *The Sports Gene: Inside the Science of Extraordinary Athletic Performance*, asked Garry Kasparov about his thought process for a move, the chess legend replied, "I see a move, a combination, almost instantly." Kasparov is able to do so based on the vast "database" of chess patterns he's built over a lifetime.

When I say "experience," I'm using the word not only in the sense of going through an event but also of having gained knowledge from it. For the latter, memory plays a fundamental role. If we had no memory, we could play the same game over and over, losing the same way every time and not getting any better. In the context of improvement, then, experience has to do with an accumulation of memories that we can use to analyze what we've done in the past and make better decisions in the future. Or better explained by writer and philosopher Aldous Huxley, "Experience is not what happens to a man; it is what a man does with what happens to him."

Chess masters have vast amounts of such memories (experience). It's what allows them to make better moves than the rest of us. And the same principle applies to other skills. Masters in all areas have practiced more, memorized more, and thus built more experience than the rest.

Efficiency

Masters make a craft look easy. They seem to perform without effort. And though part of their grace comes from having mastered the technical side of their skill, they also do less than the rest of us.

Masters exert calculated force where it matters. They use their mind and body efficiently, filtering through the unimportant, and focusing their efforts on the essential. Beginners, on the other hand, waste their energy everywhere. Novice chess players scan the entire board, considering too many moves in the hope of finding the right one (while masters concentrate on critical areas). Beginner piano players tighten their shoulders and elbows to play a note. And as a personal example, I would tense my entire body while learning salsa dancing. "Why are you tensing your arms and squeezing my hand?" my teacher used to say to me. "We are only working on foot movement!"

A good example is grappling. New students tire out after a few minutes of sparring. They are stiff, struggle for no reason, and move in all directions trying to get a better position. They also try to compensate lack of technique with brute force. But masters know when to push, pull, turn. They move with clarity, relaxing or exploding depending on the need. Good grapplers feel heavier and stronger on the mat compared to less skilled opponents with similar body types. They've learned how to use their weight and direct their force more efficiently.

Unconscious Processing

When Mihaly Csikszentmihalyi, the prominent psychologist and author of *Flow: The Psychology of Optimal Experience*, studied chess masters, he found that they had little activity in their prefrontal cortex as they played. They weren't relying on their conscious mind to make decisions. Instead, they seemed to react to patterns and sequences. They had "moved" their chess skills from the conscious mind to the faster and more efficient unconscious.

The same is true in other fields. Through practice, we progressively make our abilities subconscious, enabling them to operate "behind the scenes" and freeing up mental energy for other thinking processes—such as strategy or artistic expression. Martial artists, for instance, practice moves to the point where they no longer have to think about them, so once they are in competition, they can focus on creating openings, timing, and not getting punched in the face.

It's this "automation" of abilities that allow masters to add layers to their skill. It frees up their conscious energy to process complexity, recognize subtleties, and apply their knowledge in creative ways.

Refined Intuition

When our abilities move to the unconscious, they take on a new language. Our unconscious communicates through emotions, which are faster and less energy-demanding than conscious processing. It's the reason masters develop an intuitive "feel" for their craft and can "sense" what's happening around them. This intuition is not mystical, nor something they were born with or magically acquired; it's the result of an emotional encoding of the knowledge, patterns, and experience they've gathered over years learning their craft.

Masters' refined intuition is, in fact, a highly trained subconscious communicating with them through emotions. We all have intuition. We know what it feels like. The difference is that masters' intuition has been fine-tuned through years of experience. At their level, their craft is embedded in their way of thinking and emotional processing. As dancer Martha Graham once put it, "The body is shaped, disciplined, honored, and in time, trusted." Indeed, masters can and should trust their intuition, but the rest of us have to first develop it before we can rely on it.

Fluency and Flexibility

We consider fluency in a language to be more than knowing isolated elements such as vocabulary and grammar. Instead, it is the capacity to combine those elements to express ourselves and to interpret them in different combinations for understanding others. In the same way, masters' fluency of knowledge is not a collection of "facts" (techniques, principles, concepts) but a deeper understanding of them and their execution.

Let's use our knowledge of the alphabet as an example. We can easily say the alphabet forward (A, B, C, D, E...), but we find it hard to do it backward (Z, Y, X, W, V...). Our knowledge of the alphabet is rigid. We've always experienced it in the same direction, so that's the order we are proficient at. If we were to meet "alphabet masters," however, we'd see that their knowledge is more fluent. They could organize it forward, backward, in groups of open- or closed-mouth sounds, by the number of pen traces, or any other way. The facts do not change—the letters in the alphabet are the same—what's different is the masters' fluency in the subject.

We'll consider this depth of understanding as "fluency of knowledge," a quality all masters share regardless of their craft. For them, "the facts" become part of a web; they can be organized and combined in multiple ways, allowing for a greater range of applications.

Fluency of knowledge leads to another quality of mastery: flexibility. Masters can adjust to different situations and do so creatively if they need to. This flexibility is key for excelling at team sports, strategy games, and martial arts, for example. Those who stand out in these fields are not only technically proficient but also fluid in their approach and application. While beginners and intermediate practitioners are rigid and can only navigate limited situations, masters can succeed in almost any.

Greater Distinctions and Attention to Detail

If we were asked to identify the different elements of the *katana* (Japanese sword), most of us could only name the basics—blade, guard, handle, sheath. Well, the *katana* has over twenty elements, each with a respective name. We don't know them, but Japanese swordsmiths do. They have to. Knowing them is essential for developing their skills. With more distinctions, they get to refine both the process—how they forge the sword—and the result that comes from it, the sword itself.

In a similar way, all masters have more distinctions for what they do. They are attentive to details, which allows for a deeper understanding of their craft and more effective use of their abilities. It works as a self-feeding circle: improving in their craft makes them more aware of nuances, and becoming more aware of nuances makes them better at their craft. What's more, masters can pay attention to details without losing perspective. They can jump into the smallest things without drowning in them. They can zoom in and out as they need to, staying conscious of both the specific and the whole.

Vision-Execution Connection and Unobstructed Expression

Masters have a fine-tuned connection between vision and execution. They can materialize what they see in their mind, whether it is a movement, a painting, or a piece of writing. We can think of it as unobstructed expression. A master sculptor, for instance, can conceive an idea and then realize it in stone.

Let's use languages as an analogy one more time. We are fluent in our native language and have no barriers to express our thoughts, but when learning a foreign one, we are limited. We don't know—or can't find—the right words and have to split our focus between using correct grammar and saying what we want. It's only when we reach fluency in the new language that we can express ourselves unobstructed by the "technical" aspect of it.

The same idea applies to skills. Masters develop fluency in their technical ability to the degree that it no longer obstructs their creative expression. They fuse with their craft and the tools in it if there are any. A master cellist, for example, can feel the cello and the bow as an extension of her body, and the music she composes as an expression of her thoughts and emotions. It's what Charlie Parker wanted us to understand when he said, "Don't play the saxophone. Let it play you."

Immersion in the Craft

Charles Darwin once said, "It is a cursed evil to any man to become as absorbed in any subject as I am in mine." Indeed, this is true for masters across domains. I had the privilege of learning *Kintsugi* (the Japanese art of gold joinery) for a few days from a master of the art, Showzi Tsukamoto. When I asked him about his thoughts on *Kintsugi* and *Maki-e* (the Japanese art of gold sprinkling on *Urushi*) after over five decades practicing them, he said: "Not a moment goes by I'm not thinking about my art." His problem is not coming up with ideas for pieces. His dreams are pervaded by them. His worry is that he "won't get to make them all."

All masters fall under the same "curse" and immerse themselves in what they do—not only practicing and performing, but also studying their field in depth. Great writers don't just write a lot; they also read a lot. They analyze other writers, expand their knowledge, gather material, and study the artform. The same goes for athletes. "As a player I watched each and every game...I studied it all," says hockey legend Wayne Gretzky. And like him, many (if not all) top players and coaches in sports spend hours watching and studying games. Masters, in any field, are not only devoted practitioners of their craft but also passionate students of it.

In this chapter, we covered the different elements of mastery. We now have a better idea of what we are aiming for, as well as some requirements to get there. With that in mind, let's move on to find out what it takes to become masters ourselves.

CHAPTER 13

Path of Masters

> Only one who devotes himself to a cause with his whole strength and soul can be a true master. For this reason, mastery demands all of a person.
>
> —ALBERT EINSTEIN

Mastery shines only upon those willing to make sacrifices. It's not for the half-committed or impatient. Yet, there is nothing mystical about it. For the most part, pursuing mastery follows the same process we've discussed throughout the book: deliberate practice, gathering and using feedback, pushing our limits, and overcoming challenges. The difference is not so much in what to do, but in our attitude, involvement, and commitment to it over the years. How do we develop those? That will be the subject of this chapter. Let's explore the strategies and work ethic that will get us on the path of mastery, and the mindset to keep us in it.

Develop the Attitude of a Master to Become One

Michael Phelps' coach, Bob Bowman, used to tell him: "Are

you going to wait until after you win your gold medal to have a good attitude? No. You're going to do it beforehand. You have to have the right mental attitude and go from there. You're going to be an Olympic champion in attitude long before there's a gold medal around your neck." We need to develop the attitude and discipline of a master to become one. Medals, trophies, or awards are the recognition of a master, not the making of one. In the words of Mike Tyson, "You gotta be the champion before you wear the belt."

This change in attitude starts from deciding to become a master and committing to the process. Without making this long-term commitment, the path of mastery will elude us. No one becomes a master by chance; all great athletes, artists, and communicators have devoted themselves to their craft. "Success is no accident," the soccer great Pelé said. "It is hard work, perseverance, learning, studying, sacrifice." To become a master, we must treat our craft as a priority and give it our prime time and full energy, not leftovers.

It takes time and effort to master any craft—lots of it. There are no shortcuts, and no one else can do it for us. Everyone that has made it to the top in any field had to spend endless hours learning and refining their skill. This reality is best described by Leo Messi, another soccer superstar, who responded to praise by saying, "It took me 17 years and 114 days to become an overnight success. Starting early and staying late. Training day after day after day, year after year."

Developing the attitude of a master means being willing to put in the time and energy necessary for as long as it's necessary to achieve our goals. It also means that even if we take longer than others, or we have to put more effort than anyone else, we are still willing to do it. Masters commit to their work regardless of how difficult or how lengthy. We can take inspiration from great Renaissance artists such as Leonardo da Vinci, Michelangelo, or Lorenzo Ghiberti. They spent years, even decades, to complete their masterpieces.* For them, it wasn't about how long it would take or how hard it would be. It was about realizing their vision.

We must adopt the attitude of these masters and ask ourselves only one question, "Do I want this?" If the answer is yes, we must commit to the path, ignoring everything else. As Jiro Ono, considered by many the greatest sushi chef in the world, puts it, "Once you decide on your occupation, you must immerse yourself in your work. You have to fall in love with your work. Never complain about your job. You must dedicate your life to mastering your skill." And from the thoughts of a master in sports, we can turn to Tom Brady. When talking about having given football everything he's got, Brady said, "If you are gonna compete against me, you better be willing to give up your life, because I've given up mine." That has to be the rawest description of what it means to commit oneself to mastery. And even though that level of commitment is no guarantee we'll make it to the top, it is the only path to it—and there's no way to know how far the path will take us unless we follow it.

Efficiency to Get More, Not to Do Less

Though commitment means being willing to put in as much time and effort as necessary to reach our goals, it doesn't mean we shouldn't look for ways to optimize our approach.

---

* It took Lorenzo Ghiberti two decades to make his first set of bronze doors for Florence's Baptistery in the early fifteenth century. After their completion, he was commissioned a second set, which took him close to thirty years to complete (the doors were later referred to as "The Gates of Paradise" by Michelangelo).

Efficiency is desirable, but we must look for it with a different mindset. Most of us think of efficiency as ways to minimize time and effort and still get results. We want the fastest, easiest approach so we can do less.

Masters, and aspiring ones, also look for efficiency, but they do it to get more out of the time and energy they already put in. Their focus is on maximizing results, not on minimizing effort. In other words, they optimize their training not to cut practice or make it easier but to get more out of it. In bodybuilding, for instance, those committed to excelling look for ways to optimize their training and nutrition to speed up their progress, not ways to get away with doing the minimum. They search for efficiency to get more, not to do less.

This change in mindset is crucial. Over time, the progress of those looking for efficiency to do less remains linear. The effort decreases, but the results stay steady. It's as if someone looking to lose weight starts to exercise less because he found a program that gets him the same results with lower time investment. He'll drop weight at the same rate; he'll just be putting in less work. On the other side, the progress of those looking for efficiency to get more becomes exponential. The effort remains steady, but the results increase. In the same example, it would be as if the person looking to lose weight found a more efficient program but kept the same time investment. He will be dropping weight at a faster rate.

If we are to take the path of mastery, our search for efficiency should focus on getting the most out of our practice, not looking for ways to cut it. It's not about finding the minimum that makes the cut (how to minimize effort), but about getting the most out of the time and energy we are already committing (how to maximize results).

Observe, Study, and Emulate the Masters

We have evolved to see and copy behaviors. Observation and emulation, also known as modeling, are a fundamental and proven way to learn. We'll turn this innate ability into a strategy and model ourselves after the people we admire. We'll observe them, study what they do and how they do it, and do our best to emulate their actions.

Do not worry about losing your "style" by trying to copy the masters. We are only doing it to gain insight—to get into their heads and understand more of what they do. We can observe, study, and emulate them to refine our abilities and still be ourselves. The great Stephen King put it best when he wrote, "Don't be afraid to imitate another writer. Imitation is part of the creative process for anyone learning an art or a craft. Find the best writers in the fields that interest you and read their work aloud. Get their voice and their taste into your ear—their attitude toward language. Don't worry that by imitating them you'll lose your own voice and your own identity. Soon enough you will shed those skins and become who you are supposed to become."

Centuries before King, Benjamin Franklin applied the strategy in the hope of becoming, in his words, "a tolerable English writer." Franklin's approach was to take his favorite articles and try to recreate them from memory, "expressing each hinted sentiment at length and as fully as it had been expressed before, in any suitable words that should come to hand." He would then compare his versions to the originals to discover his faults and correct them.

Modeling is also a common practice among serious chess students. They spend a great amount of time studying the games of grandmasters move by move. They try to predict what the grandmaster would do and then analyze the move and the thinking behind it. The goal for these students is to get into the chess master's mind, see what they see, think how they think. This practice is one of the best ways for players to improve their skills.

When observing masters, we must make an effort to look beyond their performance and study their practice. If we only see them in action, we'll miss the process that took them there. It would be like seeing a magic effect and trying to replicate it without studying the method behind it. We would know the result we want to get, but we may never get it unless we learn its inner workings. In the same way, looking at masters' performances only shows us a goal to aim toward, but we need to study their practice and methods if we want to emulate them. Most of the time, as in magic, the process won't be as glamorous as the performance, but it's what we must study to become great performers ourselves.

Join the Craft's Community

Joining the craft's community means being among people with the same interest. Even athletes in individual sports train in teams or leagues. There is power in surrounding ourselves with those on the same path and who share the same passion. It allows us to exchange ideas, improve our knowledge, challenge ourselves, and discover possibilities we didn't know existed—about the field and ourselves. "When I left college to go to the pros, I thought I was the hardest-working guy," says basketball star Stephen Curry, "and seeing that firsthand [NBA guys training] was something that has changed my whole approach to the game. This whole time I thought I was pushing myself to the max...but I wasn't at the right level, and I needed to see it."

And this is as true for athletes today as it has been for intellectuals, scientists, and artists throughout history. Joining the community of our craft (as a teacher, student, colleague, teammate, admirer, or any other capacity) opens our mind to greater heights and inspires us to reach them. It also makes the journey more enjoyable.

Work with Mentors

Working with mentors is one of the best things we can do for our development. They guide us through the process, give us valuable feedback, and help us avoid unnecessary mistakes. Although there are different types of mentors—coaches, teachers, trainers, instructors—I'll refer to them simply as "mentors" to make this section easier to read.

When we work with mentors, we cut down the learning curve by taking advantage of the accumulated knowledge and experience they've gathered. We get to learn from their past mistakes and replicate what they discovered to work best. This is how we get to improve faster and ultimately advance the craft itself. Arts, sports, and other fields move forward because new generations benefit from learning and training techniques that older generations spent their careers advancing. We get to stand on the shoulders of our mentors and everyone who's influenced our domain before us.

Mentors also provide an outside perspective into our abilities. They point out problems, suggest corrections, design practice, push our limits, and provide a wealth of insight into our craft. Even the most disciplined and hardworking people will go faster through the learning process with the help of a good mentor. As a Japanese proverb reads, "Better than a thousand days of diligent study is one day with a great teacher."

I cannot overstate the value of working with mentors, regardless of our level or circumstances. Thinking we can learn and master a craft without guidance is delusional. Even the so-called prodigies from history, such as Leonardo da Vinci, Mozart, or Michelangelo, had rigorous training under accomplished and experienced instructors—Andrea del Verrocchio, Leopold Mozart, and Domenico Ghirlandaio and Bertoldo di Giovanni (the last pupil of Donatello), respectively. And from our period, all high-performance athletes work or have worked closely with coaches.

The question, then, is not if we should work with mentors—it's a must if we want to pursue mastery—but what qualities to look for in them. Here are some essential ones.

Good mentors are experienced. We need mentors who have gone through the path themselves, who've faced challenges and learned the lessons necessary to overcome them. And just as important, we need mentors who have successfully passed on those lessons to others and helped them in their path. In other words, we need mentors with experience, both as practitioners and as coaches.

Good mentors are good teachers. Teaching is a skill. Not every great performer is a great teacher; many are terrible at it. They suffer from "the curse of knowledge." This is when people are so used to doing what they do or knowing what they know that they have trouble teaching it to others. They can't put themselves in the position of someone beginning to learn what they know, so they fail to make even simple things easy to understand. Many times, we are better off learning from good teachers who are average performers than from great performers who are bad teachers. The former know how to get the best of us and make us better, while the latter only know how to do it for themselves.

Good mentors push us and give us honest feedback—even if it's hard to hear. The mentors we work with should make us stretch beyond our comfort zone, point out our mistakes, and tell us when we are slacking. They are not meant to be our compassionate friends. Their job is to make us better, which sometimes means confronting us and demanding the best we have to offer.

Good mentors are our champions. Good mentors demand the best of us because they believe we can be better and want us to be better. They are our champions—even when they don't show it. This is an important quality to look for. There's limited value in working with coaches who are half coaching us because they don't care. It's better to work with those who are willing to invest their time and energy in us, who are really "in our corner," even if they are not as accomplished.

Good mentors are obsessed with fundamentals. As we covered in the practice chapter (chapter 7), fundamentals are the essence of our craft. Good mentors are those who make us work on these fundamentals relentlessly, not those who teach us something new every time we practice. It may feel boring to work on the same things over and over—we like novelty and variety. Keep in mind, though, that it's just as boring for our mentors to see us practicing the same things time and again, but they know that's what we need to do to master our craft.

Good mentors know when not to mentor. There are moments when mentors should let us try things on our own and learn firsthand from our mistakes. Mentors who resemble overprotective parents and want to hold our hand every step of the way can be counterproductive. This is especially the case during performances. While we perform, our mind needs to be uncluttered, which means our mentors should only give us short, specific indications—if any at all, depending on the craft. Performance is not the time for them to teach us or try to correct our every move. That comes during practice or while we debrief afterward.

Good mentors are good depending on our needs. As we evolve in our craft, our needs will evolve too. The great mentor we have at the moment may not be the right person to work with months or years from now. Let's imagine you are learning to play the guitar. In the first few months, you need someone to teach you the basics: how to hold the guitar, a few chords, and some songs. You don't need the best teacher for that (though it would be great if you could work with the best from the beginning). But at further stages, you'll need someone to guide you through more specialized learning. If you are into country music, you'll need someone who can teach you the genre, the playing techniques, and how to get the sound you want.

We must value our mentors and hold them in high regard, but we also need to know when to move on. Good mentors understand this and will even encourage us to do so. They have our best interest in mind, even if that means stepping aside and letting someone else take their place. And as long as we treat our mentors with respect, value what they've done for us, and repay them by taking our craft and our path seriously, we shouldn't hesitate if the moment comes when we need to work with someone else.

So far, we've focused on the qualities of good mentors, but we have to remember that for them to be helpful, we must be good apprentices. We need to let our mentors mentor us, get our ego out of the way, and listen to what they have to say. That's why we looked for them in the first place—to get advice, direction, and guidance.

We must also keep in mind that, in the end, it's up to us

to choose our path and do the work. Mentors can't do it for us regardless of how good they are. We should seek mentors, work with them, value them, but never forget that our learning and progress are, and always will be, our responsibility, not theirs. Mentors can only guide us through the path, not walk for us or carry us through it.

As a final note, we should try to stay away from the "self-taught" route (self-directed learning is OK), and much less glorify it. Yes, it is a feat if we can get good at something on our own, but unless our circumstances prevent us from seeking out mentors to learn from and help us in our development, such avoidance is a sign of stubbornness or ego. We are being incapable of the humility required to learn from others better than us, and it will cost us. Self-teaching is slow, and it will only take us so far. Top performers have rarely mastered their craft without either the guidance or support of mentors around them.

Do the Work

Mastery is the result of progressive improvement through consistent and persistent effort. When we look at it in the short term, it doesn't take much, only a few hours of focused work a day. What's hard is doing it day after day for years. As the motto for the United States Olympic Committee reads, "It's not every four years, it's every day."

Masters work on their craft daily. It is their dedicated practice that makes them great. We could have natural abilities, motivation, an efficient method, and even great coaches, but those just optimize and encourage action; they can't substitute it. In the end, it comes down to doing the work consistently. Most writers, for example, will tell you that the hardest part about writing is not developing the plot or the characters, but having the discipline to sit down and write (and rewrite) every day.

Ambition is cheap. Motivation is cheap. The hard part is doing the groundwork. When most people find out what they need to do to reach their goals, they run away or pretend to be too busy to do them. Here is where masters (and aspiring masters) separate from everyone else: they develop the discipline to do the work.

"There's times when you are running and you just want to stop, you just wanna give up, like, to hell with this I just wanna go home." We don't imagine those words coming from Usain Bolt. We think he would show up to practice every day full of energy and motivation. No. It was difficult. It was a constant struggle. "There's days when you get up and you know that you have a training today, you know it's going to be intense and you are like, oh god I don't wanna go today," Bolt says, "but you gotta go, and it's so hard and a lot of people don't know."

Bolt kept showing up every day for years, even when his "conscience" would tell him, "Don't do it, stop running, retire, go play football, go play golf." That's the "secret" of masters, relentless work ethic. They do the work whether they feel like it or not, whether they are inspired or not, if they are tired or not, if everyone else is taking a day off or not. It doesn't change. They just do it. Every. Single. Day.

One Day at a Time

Most of the time, "doing the work" should be something we take on with passion and enjoy making part of our lives. But pursuing mastery won't always be enjoyable. There will be days or weeks when we don't want to practice. Our progress will seem too slow and the road too long. We need to be ready to go through these phases and still show up ready to give our all.

One way to stay consistent is by taking things one day at a time. This is a proven psychological strategy to overcome one of the most intense challenges a human being can endure: addiction. Recovery programs talk about "winning the day," an approach that encourages focusing on today—the here and now. Alcoholics, for instance, are taught to direct their thinking to "I won't drink today" and avoid obsessing about what happened yesterday or what may happen tomorrow.

Paying attention to the present moment removes the weight from the number of days they have been recovering and the pressure of having to stay sober for years to come. Thinking, "I won't drink for the rest of my life," is overwhelming, even scary. But if the goal is "I won't drink today," it becomes manageable, realistic, doable. And once achieved, it's a matter of renewing it day after day for months, years, and hopefully, a lifetime.

Recovering from addiction is an extreme example, but it sheds light into our psychology. Projecting work into the future can discourage us from doing it, but breaking it down into daily actionable steps will empower us. The greatest feats can be achieved if we shorten the timeframes and take it one day at a time.

With the respect and admiration that recovering addicts deserve, we'll use their example as inspiration for achieving our own goals. We'll borrow their strategy of short-term attention for long-term success to stay on the path of mastery. Rather than thinking, "I'll practice hard day after day for the next five or ten years," we'll think, "I'll practice hard today."

We'll avoid looking back at how much we've already practiced, which can make us want to take a break, or looking forward to how much more we have to do, which can be discouraging. We'll focus instead on what we can do today to take a step closer to our goals. And that's all that matters: progressive improvement through consistent and persistent effort over time, the foundation of mastery.

Even with this strategy, we may feel as if the level of discipline and dedication required from us is out of reach. So, it's important to mention that it gets more manageable with time. Part of it comes from building momentum and habit—the more we do the work, the easier it is to keep doing it—and another part comes from getting better. As we improve in our craft, we start a self-feeding cycle that motivates us to keep working at it. The more we practice, the better we get, and the better we get, the more we want to practice. This cycle takes some time to get going, but once it does, it'll help us sustain the day-to-day work in the long term.

No Compromises

In pursuing mastery, we need to develop the habit of keeping our effort all the way to the end in anything we do. In sports, this means playing the last minutes of a game with the same intensity we gave it throughout—whether we are winning by a landslide or losing with no chance of recovery. The score and the expiring clock are not reasons to pull back. We must give everything down to the end.

Think of Formula One legend Michael Schumacher. On some occasions, he had a world title secured early in the season, but he refused to lower his standards. He would come out, Grand Prix after Grand Prix, racing with as much urgency as if the championship was still on the line. No race went too well to slow down, none so badly as to warrant giving up. Schumacher raced with a commitment to giving his best every day no matter what.

From a different field, we can look at a master of writing and my favorite author, Robert Greene. He spent close to a decade researching and writing his magnum opus, *The Laws of Human Nature*. Aside from the time and energy commitment, the project also took a toll on his health. Many in his position would have given in to the pull of taking shortcuts and just being done with the book. But not Greene. Every chapter, every story, every quote, every detail is deliberate. No shortcuts. No compromises. Quality all the way to the end.

There's a popular saying these days that goes, "Done is better than perfect." Sure, the search for perfection is a lost cause and often a form of procrastination caused by fear. But rushing to the end is just as problematic if done to avoid the hard work. Perfection shouldn't be our goal—that's a trap—but neither should be completion for its own sake. Cutting to the finish line to get things over with is mediocre. What we should be after is putting our best effort from beginning to end, making sure we don't sacrifice the quality of the process regardless of difficulty, length, or frustration.

That's the attitude of masters. They are aware of the black hole they can fall into if they go after perfection. But they also know that "done" means nothing if it's not done right. Good enough is not good enough for them. What they strive for is "best-ism," doing their best given their current abilities, which is all anyone can ever do. So, while perfectionism is about trying to be perfect, an impossible task, "best-ism" is about asking ourselves, "Does this work reflect the best of my current abilities?" If not, we must keep improving it. We'll only move on when we know we made no compromises, no sacrifice in our standards, and gave our best until there was no steam left, even if far from perfect.

Process Over Outcomes

We tend to obsess about outcomes. In sports, it's winning a game or competition; in arts, it could be good reviews or appreciation. There's nothing wrong with wanting those things, but if we fixate on them, we end up taking our attention away from what makes them possible—the process.

We must prioritize process over outcome every time, pouring our energy into what's in front of us and doing it to the best of our ability, step by step. That, incidentally, makes it more likely we will get the outcomes we want: winning, giving an amazing performance, or creating outstanding work. Quality in the process leads to quality in the outcomes.

For a performing musician, this means concentrating on playing each song as best as possible instead of wondering about the public's opinion. And for athletes in team sports, it would be focusing on each play instead of thinking of the score or how much they want to win. In the words of legendary coach Phil Jackson, "Obsessing about winning is a loser's game: the most we can hope for is to create the best possible conditions for success, then let go of the outcome."

Another reason not to fixate on results is that, in some cases, they are influenced by factors beyond our control. In sports, we can't control the element of luck or what our opponent is doing. If we only look at outcomes, whether we won or lost, we can end up with wrong assessments of our performance and abilities. "Good" outcomes can lead to feelings of grandeur, keeping us from seeing our mistakes and opportunities for growth. And on the other side, "bad" outcomes can lead to low morale, preventing us from seeing what we did right and priding ourselves for having given our best. When all we care about is outcomes, we live or die with the "score" and become blind to the big picture.

This is not to say we shouldn't care about outcomes. They are important. They give us a sense of direction, a target to aim at. And for most of us, they are the reason—and motivation—for getting into a craft. But to have the best chances of getting our desired outcomes, we must focus on the process instead. Our attention during practice or performance should be on the task at hand; the results will take care of themselves. As football coach Nick Saban would tell his players: "Don't think about winning the SEC Championship. Don't think about the National Championship. Think about what you needed to do in this drill, on this play, in this moment. That's the process: Let's think about what we can do today, the task at hand."*

Make Progress the Main Goal

Improvement must always be our main goal. Success, winning, admiration, and recognition can look great, but we need to remember that they are a result of getting better over time. Michael Phelps offers us insight into this thinking: "I discovered something about myself early on too. I could be motivated not just by winning. By improving my strokes. Hitting split times. Setting records. Doing my best times. There was any number of things I could do to get better. Winning

---

* As reported by Ryan Holiday in his wonderful book *The Obstacle Is the Way: The Timeless Art of Turning Trials into Triumph.*

never gets old, but there was a way to win that showed I was getting better, and could get better still."

We sometimes forget that great achievements come from small improvements compounded over time. By going after progress at every step and on every aspect of his craft, Phelps was making winning an inevitable consequence of the process. We must follow his example and keep our aim on being better than yesterday or the week before. Striving for progress is what ultimately leads to all other outcomes.

Take Risks

Those willing to take risks, make mistakes, and fail eventually make it further than the rest. As Muhammad Ali said, "He who is not courageous enough to take risks will accomplish nothing in life." In figure skating, the best skaters are willing to fall more often. They push their abilities to the edge and work on jumps they are not good at. That's why they fall, and that's why they rise to the top. And from a different domain, we can turn to Michael Jordan's famous words, "I've missed more than 9,000 shots in my career. I've lost almost 300 games. Twenty-six times I've been trusted to take the game-winning shot and missed. I've failed over and over and over again in my life. And that is why I succeed."

Masters are willing to try things, take risks, and go to the edge of their skills. That means making mistakes and failing, sometimes even looking foolish. It is hard work, both mentally and physically, but it's the path we must follow. And if discouraged for failing, again and again, we can find comfort in the words of Teddy Roosevelt:

It is not the critic who counts; not the man who points out how the strong man stumbles, or where the doer of deeds could have done them better. The credit belongs to the man who is actually in the arena, whose face is marred by dust and sweat and blood; who strives valiantly; who errs, who comes short again and again, because there is no effort without error and shortcoming; but who does actually strive to do the deeds; who knows great enthusiasms, the great devotions; who spends himself in a worthy cause; who at the best knows in the end the triumph of high achievement, and who at the worst, if he fails, at least fails while daring greatly, so that his place shall never be with those cold and timid souls who neither know victory nor defeat.

We may fail, but we are failing in a path of greatness that most will never have the courage to take.

Overcome Success

We don't think of success as a challenge. Reaching goals usually works as a motivator to keep pushing forward. But sometimes, especially after hitting a significant goal, success can make us fall into one of several traps that slows down or even stops our progress: complacency, overconfidence, or fear.

Complacency comes from becoming comfortable with our skills and not pushing hard to improve them anymore. It's when we reach a milestone and make it our comfort zone. We choose to be proficient at our level over being clumsy and frustrated trying to reach a higher one. It can also take the form of feeling that we earned a break, that we can take it easy for a while. We say to ourselves, "I've done well. I don't need to work at it today. I can take some days off." But how can we expect to keep improving or even maintaining the level we've reached if we ease on the very training that took us there?

Complacency has no place in the search for mastery. We need to stay hungry and continue pushing to greater heights. An example to bring back is Tiger Woods. He changed an already-great swing because he thought it could not take him where he wanted to go. "People thought it was asinine for me to change my swing after I won the Masters by twelve shots," Woods said to an interviewer. "Why would you want to change that? Well, I thought I could become better." It took him a long time to develop his new swing, and he had to stand losses and criticism while he did it. But it eventually paid off, and he became a better golfer because of it.

Overconfidence, also considered as ego, pride, or entitlement, comes from believing we no longer need to do the work. We think we are too good to practice or prepare, that those things are beneath us. This usually happens when we reach a major goal. We start feeling like we've "made it," and, with everyone around us celebrating our success and telling us how good we are, our ego grows out of proportion. Overconfidence makes us cut down our practice, take more breaks, ease our standards, and lose focus. As a result, our skills stall or decline.

We must fight overconfidence with humbleness. The path of mastery requires that we remind ourselves that there is always more to improve. It also needs constant attention and maintenance. Our skills are not a "get it and forget it" deal; we have to work on them to keep them sharp. In the words of "The Perfect Violinist," Jascha Heifetz: "If I don't practice one day, I know it; two days, the critics know it; three days, the public knows it."

If we find ourselves thinking we are too good, a way to regain humbleness is to watch and study our idols. They are a great reminder that there's more path ahead, and we should get back to work. For those in sports, a good way to come down from the cloud is to compete against someone better. There's nothing like an up-close and personal challenge—and loss—to put our ego back in check.

Another option is simply to go back to "the grind." When we take a break after reaching an important milestone or having success, we may start believing that we got our results because of how great we are. And that success will continue to roll because, well, we "deserve it." We lose perspective of what it took to get there and what it'll take to stay there or go beyond. Going back to work counters this detachment from reality. Hard work is humbling; it reminds us that whatever success we achieved came at a price and that we shouldn't take it for granted—and above all, that we shouldn't expect things to get easier or have a free pass based on our past glories.

Pursuing mastery demands that we let our successes expire and imagine we start every project, every training camp, every competition anew and prove ourselves again. "You win a race, the next race it's a question mark. Are you still the best or not?" Those were Michael Schumacher's thoughts during his racing career. "That's what is funny. But that's what is interesting. And that's what is challenging. You have to prove yourself every time." This is not to say that we shouldn't enjoy or be proud of our successes, but that we must not expect them to carry us forever or think they exempt us from doing the work. Our efforts need to be renewed time and again, regardless of how much we have achieved in the past.

Fear is another challenge of success, especially when our achievements put us under public scrutiny. We become afraid of not being able to top what we've done, or not living up to our past standards and having to face criticism because of it.

We begin to doubt our abilities and avoid taking risks, choosing to stick to what worked in the past instead, which moves us closer to the stagnation we fear. As Pablo Picasso argued, "Success is dangerous. One begins to copy oneself, and to copy oneself is more dangerous than to copy others."

The pressure to replicate, and even outdo, our past successes can lead to mental blocks and even neglecting the craft. One of the best ways to overcome this challenge is to stay present and do the work in front of us while ignoring the noise. This means committing fully to the process and keeping our attention on doing the task at hand to the best of our ability, instead of dwelling on imagined outcomes or criticism.

Remember, we'll eventually experience success and, with it, new types of challenges: complacency, overconfidence, fear. We can't let them derail us. We'll combat complacency by staying hungry, overconfidence by staying humble, and fear by staying focused on the process.

Kaizen (改善)

Kaizen is the Japanese word for improvement. It also refers to a business philosophy of continuous betterment that originated in Japan and has now transcended into self-development around the world. As a personal philosophy, *Kaizen* stands for living an examined life and making continuous changes to improve it, while embracing that there will always be more to work on. If there were a philosophy that could come close to encompassing mastery, *Kaizen* would be it—the never-ending pursuit of improvement.

Becoming a master requires that we never feel like one. Others may call us that, but we should never do so ourselves. We must forever remain apprentices. All masters know there is more to do, more to learn, more to improve. They remain devoted students of their craft and of themselves.

An embodiment of this philosophy is sushi master Jiro Ono, "Even after working at sushi restaurants for 50 years, I don't believe I've mastered sushi yet," Ono-san says. "Every day, while working, I am constantly thinking there is much more to do." *Kaizen*, the philosophy of an endless search for improvement, defines the path of all true masters—the path that awaits us.

Closing Thoughts

I work harder than anyone who has ever lived.
—MICHELANGELO

Michelangelo completed his *Pietà* when he was twenty-four. We would think that carving such a masterpiece would be the highest point of his career, but it was only the beginning. For the next sixty years, Michelangelo pushed his skills to produce masterpieces in painting, sculpture, and architecture.

The myth around Michelangelo, however, the magic we wish existed, the ease with which we believe greatness came to him is nothing of the sort. He had a slow start, wasn't considered a prodigy, and for every masterpiece he made, there were numerous unfinished, uninspired, or abandoned works.

Michelangelo was all too human, but he gave all his humanity to his art. Once committed to a project, he would immerse himself in it, neglecting sociability and even health. "I have no friends of any sort and want none. I haven't even time enough to eat as I should," he wrote to his brother while working on the Sistine Chapel ceiling, "so you mustn't bother

me with anything else, for I could not bear another thing."*
And when asked about not having a family, Michelangelo replied, "I've always had only too harassing a wife in this demanding art of mine, and the works I leave behind will be my sons."

That was the source of Michelangelo's mastery: absolute devotion to his craft. Even in old age, as his body withered, his health declined, and the strength of his hands abandoned him, Michelangelo remained faithful to his work. He spent the last seventeen years of his life on the construction of St. Peter's Basilica. And days before his death, weeks short of turning eighty-nine, he continued to work on a sculpture.†

Art was his job, his passion, his leisure, his legacy—what the Japanese would call his *Ikigai* (reason to live). And he dedicated himself to mastering it from the moment he began his training until his last breath eighty years later.

Whether your goal is to become a master like Michelangelo, take on a new craft as a hobby, or get better at a skill you already practice, you now know the path to get there. You won't be held back by false beliefs about talent or the common challenges that prevent most people from pursuing a passion.

It's time to become the artist, athlete, or professional you've always wanted to be, and now you have the tools to make that happen. You know the process, understand the principles, and possess the strategies to learn, improve, and master your craft.

You hold the method to create the *"magic."*

---

* Goethe would later write about the work, "Until you have seen the Sistine Chapel, you can have no adequate conception of what man is capable of accomplishing."

† The so-called *Rondanini Pietà*.

Encore?

If you enjoyed *Learn, Improve, Master* and want more, here's some bonus material I prepared for you:

- **Bonus Chapter: The "Renaissance Man" Revisited.** I couldn't fit this chapter in the book—though it's one of my favorites. It's an approach to learning from multiple domains and combining them.
- **Collection of Quotes.** During my research, I gathered great quotes on knowledge, learning, overcoming challenges, and mastery. I added many to the book but had to leave out many others. This is the entire collection organized by theme.
- **Conversation with a Kintsugi Master.** This is my conversation with Showzi Tsukamoto (the *Kintsugi* master mentioned in chapter 12) about his art and his journey.

Get the FREE bonuses at:

UnlimitedMastery.com/LIMbonus

Also, if you want more on learning, practicing, habits, goal setting, mastery, and all other subjects in this book, you can subscribe to my free newsletter and get my latest articles directly in your inbox. Subscribers also get special reports and a first look at new projects I'm working on. You can sign up at:

UnlimitedMastery.com/newsletter

Lastly, I would love to hear about your journey, your favorite strategies, and if I can help you overcome any challenge. Let's connect on Instagram or Twitter: **@velznick**.

Acknowledgments

> If I have seen further it is by standing on the shoulders of giants.
>
> —ISAAC NEWTON

All my life, I've benefited from the hard work of great minds who have dedicated their lives to improving our understanding of the world and ourselves. I would like to start by thanking them. To the scientists, scholars, researchers, and thinkers who have elevated our collective wisdom—thank you, this book stands on your contribution.

To all masters, thank you for pushing the perceived limits of our capabilities. Your devotion to your craft, and mastery of it, makes us dream and stand in awe of the human potential. You were the inspiration for this book.

To the country and people of Japan, I have the most admiration for your culture and way of life. I can't be grateful enough for everything you've given me. You were there for me in my darkest times and brought me back to life. Thank you for being all the amazing things you are.

To Robert Greene, thank you for being a role model and

setting a standard that all non-fiction writers should try to live up to, both in depth of research and quality of prose. Your example was a guiding force to keep improving my writing and my work.

To Ryan Holiday, thank you for the advice on writing and publishing. And above all, thank you for writing your book *Perennial Seller*. It was my source of wisdom for shaping, improving, and completing this project. It also encouraged me to give it my best, even during the dreadful moments when all I wanted was to be done with it.

To Ann, without your insight and contribution this book would be a rant on learning science. Thank you for helping me shape a clear vision and keeping me in line with it. I also want to thank you for pushing me to become a better writer, and for having my back all the times I wasn't.

To the Scribe Publishing team, thank you for your amazing service and support. I've worked with many companies across industries, and I have never seen a team of professionals with your level of organization. You've mastered the multidisciplinary and complex process of helping authors publish their books. Thank you for working with me.

To my family: Mom, thank you for all the sacrifices you made so I could have a better life. You've been the greatest. I love you. Dad, thank you for showing me what it is to live honorably down to the last breath. You are my hero. Camilo, thank you for taking care of me and being my best friend through all these years. I couldn't ask for a better brother.

To Paula, no amount of words will do justice to everything you mean to me. You've always supported everything I've done, even the unconventional and surreal. Thank you for so many years of encouragement and unconditional love. I don't want a life without you in it.

To you, the reader, time is life; thank you for entrusting part of your life to me. My greatest hope is that the value you got from this book was worth the time you invested in it. Thank you for reading.

About the Author

NICK VELASQUEZ is a passionate learner and devoted student of mastery. He's the author of the popular blog UnlimitedMastery.com, where he writes about learning science, peak performance, creativity, and mastering skills. His writing has been featured in outlets such as *TIME* and *Thought Catalogue*. Nick speaks multiple languages and spends his time between Tokyo and Montréal.

Selected Bibliography

> Our knowledge is the amassed thought and experience of innumerable minds.
>
> —RALPH WALDO EMERSON

Brown, Peter, Henry Roediger III, and Mark McDaniel. *Make it Stick. The Science of Successful Learning.* Cambridge: Belknap/Harvard, 2014.

Carey, Benedict. *How We Learn: The Surprising Truth About When, Where, and Why it Happens.* New York: Random House, 2015.

Novak, Joseph, and Bob Gowin. *Learning How to Learn.* United Kingdom: Cambridge University Press, 2008.

Doyle, Terry, and Todd Zakrajsek. *The New Science of Learning: How to Learn in Harmony With Your Brain.* Sterling, Virginia: Stylus, 2013.

Sousa, David. *How the Brain Learns.* 4th ed. Thousand Oaks, CA: Corwin, 2011.

Knud, Illeris. *Contemporary Theories of Learning: Learning Theorists...in Their Own Words.* New York: Routledge, 2009.

Blakemore, Sarah-Jayne, and Uta Frith. *The Learning Brain: Lessons for Education.* Malden, MA: Blackwell, 2005.

Illeris, Knud. *How We Learn: Learning and Non-learning in School and Beyond*. New York: Routledge, 2007.

Ambrose, Susan, Michael Bridges, Michele DiPietro, Marsha Lovett, and Marie Normal. *How Learning Works: 7 Research-based Principles for Smart Teaching*. San Francisco, CA: Jossey-Bass, 2010.

Boser, Ulrich. *Learn Better: Mastering The Skills for Success in Life, Business, and School, or How to Become an Expert in Just About Anything*. New York: Rodale, 2017.

Kahneman, Daniel. *Thinking Fast and Slow*. Canada: Doubleday, 2011.

Medina, John. *Brain Rules: 12 Principles for Surviving and Thriving at Work, Home, and School*. Seattle: Pear press, 2009.

Doidge, Norman. *The Brain That Changes Itself: Stories of Personal Triumph From the Frontiers of Brain Science*. New York: Penguin, 2007.

Treffert, Darold. *Island of Genius: The Bountiful Mind of The Autistic, Acquired, and Sudden Savant*. Philadelphia, PA: Jessica Kingsley, 2012.

Hawkins, Jeff, and Sandra Blakeslee. *On Intelligence: How a New Understanding of the Brain Will Lead to the Creation of Truly Intelligent Machines*. New York: St. Martin's Griffin, 2004.

Lilienfeld, Scott, Seven Jay Lynn, John Ruscio, and Barry L. Beyerstein. *50 Great Myths of Popular Psychology: Shattering Widespread Misconceptions About Human Behavior*. United Kingdom: Wiley-Blackwell, 2010.

Martin, Paul. *Counting Sheep: The Science and Pleasures of Sleep and Dreams*. United Kingdom: Flamingo, 2003.

Campayo, Ramon. *Desarrolle una mente prodigiosa*. Madrid, Spain: Edaf, 2004.

Campayo, Ramon. *Aprende un idioma en 7 días*. Madrid, Spain: Edaf, 2006.

Wyner, Gabriel. *Fluent Forever: How to Learn any Language Fast and Never Forget it*. New York: Harmony, 2014.

Lewis, Benny. *Fluent in 3 Months: How Anyone at any Age Can Learn a Language From Anywhere in The World*. Harper Collins, 2014.

Buzan, Tony. *Use Your Head: How to Unleash the Power of Your Mind*. Great Britain: BBC, 2010.

Buzan, Tony and Barry Buzan. *The Mind Map Book: Unlock Your Creativity, Boost Your Memory, Change Your Life*. Great Britain: BBC, 2010.

Buzan, Tony. *The Memory Book: How to Remember Anything You Want*. Great Britain: BBC, 2010.

Yates, Frances. *The Art of Memory*. United Kingdom: Pimlico, 2010.

Horsley, Kevin. *Unlimited Memory: How to Use Advanced Learning Strategies to Learn Faster, Remember More, and Be More Productive*. TCK Publishing, 2016.

Joer, Joshua. *Moonwalking With Einstein: The Art and Science of Remembering Everything*. New York: Penguin, 2011.

Schacter, Daniel. *The Seven Sins of Memory: How the Mind Forgets and Remembers*. New York: Houghton Mifflin, 2002.

O'Brian, Dominic. *How to Develop a Perfect Memory*. United Kingdom: Pavilion, 1993.

Higbee, Kenneth. *Your Memory: How it Works & How to Improve it*. Boston: Da Capo Press, 2001.

Lorayne, Harry. *How to Develop a Super Power Memory*. Hollywood, FL: Fell, 1990.

Heath, Chip, and Dan Heath. *Made to Stick: Why Some Ideas Survive and Others Die*. New York: Random House, 2008.

Rubin, Gretchen. *Better Than Before: Mastering the Habits of Our Everyday Lives*. Canada: Doubleday, 2015.

Duhigg, Charles. *The Power of Habit: Why We Do What We Do in Life and Business*. Canada: Doubleday, 2012.

Dean, Jeremy. *Making Habits, Breaking Habits. Why We Do Things, Why We Don't, and How to Make any Change Stick*. Boston: Da Capo Press, 2013.

Clear, James. *Atomic Habits: An Easy & Proven Way to Build Good Habits & Break Bad Ones*. New York: Avery, 2018.

Heath, Chip, and Dan Heath. *Switch: How to Change Things When Change is Hard*. New York: Random House, 2010.

Wiseman, Richard. *:59 Seconds: Think a Little, Change a Lot*. United Kingdom: Pan Books, 2010.

Baumeister, Roy, and John Tierney. *Willpower: Rediscovering the Greatest Human Strength*. New York: Penguin, 2011.

Ericsson, Anders and Robert Pool. *Peak: How all of us Can Achieve Extraordinary Things*. Toronto, Canada: Penguin Canada, 2017.

Ericsson, Anders K. Neil Charness, Paul J. Feltovich, and Robert R. Hoffman, eds. *The Cambridge Handbook of Expertise and Expert Performance*. United Kingdom: Cambridge University Press, 2006.

Chipman, Susan, Judith Segal, and Robert Glasser, eds. *Thinking and Learning Skills Volume 2: Research and Open Questions*. New York: Routledge, 1985.

Farrow, Damian, Joseph Baker, and Clare MacMahon, eds. *Developing Sport Expertise: Researchers and Coaches Put Theory Into Practice*. New York: Routledge, 2013.

Lemov, Doug, Erica Woolway, and Katie Yezzi. *Practice Perfect: 42 Rules for Getting Better at Getting Better*. San Francisco: Jossey-Bass, 2012.

Sterner, Thomas. *The Practicing Mind: Developing Focus and Discipline in Your Life*. Novato, CA: New World Library, 2012.

Coyle, Daniel. *The Little Book of Talent: 52 Tips for Improving Your Skills*. New York: Bantam, 2012.

Coyle, Daniel. *The Talent Code: Greatness Isn't Born. It's Grown. Here's How.* New York: Bantam Dell, 2009.

Waitzkin, Josh. *The Art of Learning: An Inner Journey to Optimal Performance.* New York: Free Press, 2007.

Kaufman, Josh. *The First 20 Hours: How to Learn Anything Fast.* New York: Penguin, 2013.

Ferris, Timothy. *The 4-hour Chef: The Simple Path to Cooking Like a Pro, Learning Anything, and Living the Good Life.* New York: New Harvest, 2012.

Ferris, Timothy. *Tools of Titans: The Tactics, Routines, and Habits of Billionaires, Icons, and World-class Performers.* New York: Houghton Mifflin Harcourt, 2017.

Epstein, David. *The Sports Gene: Inside the Science of Extraordinary Athletic Performance.* New York: Portfolio/Penguin, 2014.

Epstein, David. *Range: Why Generalists Triumph in a Specialized World.* New York: Riverhead Books, 2019.

Csikszentmihalyi, Mihaly. *Creativity: The Psychology of Discovery and Invention.* New York: Harper Perennial, 2013.

Csikszentmihalyi, Mihaly. *Flow: The Psychology of Optimal Experience.* New York: Harper Perennial, 2008.

Dweck, Carol. *Mindset: The New Psychology of Success.* New York: Random House, 2006.

Duckworth, Angela. *Grit: The Power of Passion and Perseverance.* Canada: Collins, 2018.

Kotler, Steven. *The Rise of Superman: Decoding the Science of Ultimate Human Performance.* New York, New Harvest, 2014.

Syed, Matthew. *Bounce: Mozart, Federer, Picasso, Beckham, and the Science of Success.* New York: HarperCollins, 2010.

LeUnes, Arnold. *Sport Psychology: A Practical Guide*. United Kingdom: Icon Books, 2011.

Afremow, Jim. *The Champion's Mind: How Great Athletes Think, Train, and Thrive*. New York: Rodale, 2014.

Verstegen, Mark. *Every Day is Game Day: The Proven System of Elite Performance to Win All Day, Every Day*. New York: Penguin, 2014.

Mack, Gary, and David Casstevens. *Mind Gym: An Athlete's Guide to Inner Excellence*. New York: McGraw-Hill, 2001.

Mcguinness, Mark. *Resilience: Facing Down Rejection & Criticism on the Road to Success*. Lateral Action, 2012.

Babineaux, Ryan and John Krumboltz. *Fail Fast, Fail Often: How Losing Can Help You Win*. New York: Penguin, 2013.

Maltz, Maxwell. *The New Psycho-Cybernetics: The Original Science of Self-Improvement and Success That Has Changed the Lives of Over 30 Million People*. Prentice Hall Press, New York 2001.

Brown, Jeff, Mark Fenske, and Liz Neporent. *The Winner's Brain: 8 Strategies Great Minds Use to Achieve Success*. Boston: Da Capo Press, 2010.

Fader, Jonathan. *Life as Sport: What Top Athletes Can Teach You About How to Win in Life*. Boston: Da Capo Press, 2016.

Stulberg, Brad and Steve Magness. *Peak Performance: Elevate Your Game, Avoid Burnout, and Thrive With The New Science of Success*. New York: Rodale, 2017.

Hof, Wim and Justin Rosales. *Becoming the Iceman: Pushing Past Perceived Limits*. Minneapolis, MN: Mill City Press, 2012.

Selk, Jason. *10-minute toughness: The Mental-training Program for Winning Before the Game Begins*. New York: McGraw-Hill, 2009.

Lynch, Jerry and Chungliang Al Huang. *The Way of The Champion: Lessons From Sun Tzu's The Art of War and Other Tao Wisdom for Sports and Life*. North Clarendon: Tuttle, 2006.

Grover, Tim. *Relentless: From Good to Great to Unstoppable*. New York: Scribner, 2014.

Ledbetter, Brett. *What Drives Winning*. WDW Publishing, 2015.

Pressfield, Steven. *The War of Art: Break Through the Blocks and Win Your Inner Creative Battles*. New York: Black Irish Entertainment LLC, 2002.

Robichaud, Melisa and Kristin Buhr. *The Worry Workbook: CBT Skills to Overcome Worry & Anxiety by Facing the Fear of Uncertainty*. Oakland, CA: New Harbinger Publications, 2018.

Evans, Dylan. *Placebo: Mind Over Matter in Modern Medicine*. United Kingdom: Oxford University Press, 2004

Willink, Jocko and Leif Babin. *Extreme Ownership: How U.S. Navy SEALs Lead and Win*. New York: St. Martin's Press, 2017.

Leonard, George. *Mastery: The Keys to Success and Long-term Fulfilment*. New York: Penguin, 1992.

Jackson, Phil, and Hugh Delehanty. *Eleven Rings: The Soul of Success*. New York: Penguin, 2013.

Jordan, Michael. *I Can't Accept Not Trying*. San Francisco, CA: HarperCollins, 1994.

Phelps, Michael, and Alan Abrahamson. *No Limits: The Will to Succeed*. New York: Free Press, 2008.

Shamrock, Frank and Charles Fleming. *Uncaged: My life as a Champion MMA Fighter*. Chicago: Chicago Review Press, 2012.

Lamott, Anne. *Bird by Bird: Some Instructions on Writing and Life*. New York: Anchor Books, 1995.

King, Stephen. *On Writing: A Memoir of the Craft*. New York: Scribner, 2000.

Larry W. Phillips, ed. *Ernest Hemingway on Writing*. New York: Scribner, 2004.

Martin Kemp, ed. *Leonardo On Painting*, translated by Margaret Walker. New Haven: Yale University Press, 1989.

Eduards, Betty. *Drawing on the Right Side of the Brain: A Course in Enhancing Creativity and Artistic Confidence*. New York. Tarcher/Penguin, 2012.

Brown, D.W. *You Can Act!: A Complete Guide For Actors*. Studio City: Michael Wise Productions, 2009.

Hearst, Eliot, and John Knott. *Blindfold Chess: History, Psychology, Techniques, Champions, World Records, and Important Games*. Jefferson: McFarland, 2009.

Currey, Mason. *Daily Rituals: How Artists Work*. New York: Alfred A. Knopf, 2014.

Holiday, Ryan and Stephen Hanselman. *The Daily Stoic: 366 Meditations on Wisdom, Perseverance, and The Art of Living*. New York: Portfolio/Penguin, 2016.

Holiday, Ryan. *The Obstacle is the Way. The Timeless Art of Turning Trials Into Triumph*. New York: Portfolio/Penguin, 2014.

Holiday, Ryan. *Ego is the Enemy*. New York: Portfolio/Penguin, 2016.

Brown, Derren. *Happy: Why More or Less Everything is Absolutely Fine*. United Kingdom: Bantam Press, 2016.

Brown, Derren. *Tricks of the Mind*. United Kingdom: Channel 4 books, 2007.

Greene, Robert and 50 cent. *The 50th law*. New York: HarperCollins, 2009.

Greene, Robert. *The Laws of Human Nature*. New York: Viking, 2018.

Greene, Robert. *Mastery*. New York: Viking, 2012.

Ono, Jiro. *Jiro Philosophy*. Japan: Shogagukan, 2016.

Fujimoto, Mari. *Ikigai & Other Japanese Words to Live By*. United Kingdom: Modern Books, 2019.

Aurelius, Marcus. *Meditations,* translated by Gregory Hays. New York: Modern Library, 2003.

Nietzsche, Friedrich. *Human, All Too human,* translated by R.J. Hollingday. United Kingdom: Cambridge University Press, 1996.

Suchet, John. *Mozart: The Man Revealed*. New York: Pegasus Books, 2017.

Isaacson, Walter. *Leonardo da Vinci*. New York: Simon & Schuster, 2017.

Wallace, William E. *Michelangelo: The artist, The man, and His Times*. United Kingdom: Cambridge University Press, 2010.